EXORCISING MY DEMONS

An Actress' Journey to The Exorcist and Beyond

By

Eileen Dietz
&
Daniel Loubier

ISBN: 978-0-9852146-8-5
Library of Congress Control Number: 2013900107

First Published by *AuthorMike Dark Ink*, 3/18/2013

www.AuthorMikeInk.com

AuthorMike Ink, AuthorMike *Dark Ink* and its logos are trademarked by *AuthorMike Ink*.

Printed in the United States of America

To Thomas Albany
Who has put up with me all these years

and

Chris Roe
To whom I owe so much

TABLE OF CONTENTS

CHAPTER ONE

"I see good fortune for you, the answer to all your dreams, Cameras and film." Mrs. Carvainis, the Medium told me. She could have been hired by Central Casting to play the part of the quintessential spiritualist. "If you keep to your present path" she continued, "you will reach the top of your field. Right now I feel contracts and money. Lots of money. But be careful. There are negative forces. Everything will begin to happen in a festive atmosphere. I see cameras and people. But keep your faith at all times because there are forces trying to tear you down, Demonic forces. Trust to whatever you believe in," she continued. *"You must see both sides of what you are doing in order to take the right path. Satan wears many disguises and can easily fool you. Some people think the devil doesn't exist, just as some people think God is dead. It's your choice."*

Ah, if only I had listened, the course of my history would have been so different."

- From *Fifty Cents for Your Soul*, by Denise Dietz

This book is about dreams. Dreams so big and so strong that nothing can push them aside. More specifically, it's about the dream of a small, buck-toothed, flat-chested girl from

Queens-by-way-of-New York City and how against all odds and sentiments, she still managed to get herself cast in the scariest movie of all time.

It's also about choices--some bad, others that were simply life-changers. Some nights when I'm lying in bed and can't sleep, I think about the ones that were *really bad*. Of the incredibly poor choices, people tell me they must have seemed like the right thing to do at the time. To those people I say, "Not so much…" Wise men (and even some friends of mine) like to say, "No choices are bad; it is the journey you are on and what you learn from those choices that make you who you are." I would have preferred my lessons to be learned a bit easier but sometimes you make a choice because, in that moment, it feels like the right one. Other times, you make a choice *knowing* you should do the opposite.

These days I believe in something I like to call my "God nudge." It's that little feeling in your gut that says, "Uh oh, not so fast," right before you're about to do something stupid. It's the part of us that knows when we're going down the wrong path, but it gets ignored for whatever reason. Sadly, we don't always listen to this nudge and we stubbornly go our own way. Of this, I am surely guilty.

Greed is certainly one reason for making a poor choice. A friend of mine--another actress--once insisted on having her name appear above the title of a film she starred in based on the terms that had been agreed upon. She ended up getting her name above the title and the film went on to be a huge success. Unfortunately, due to her "Me!" attitude, my friend got blacklisted. I also believe bad choices are (more likely) made out of some inordinate need for attention or some fear of being ignored. "Hey, it's me! Look over here! It's Eileen! Look this way!" As a child growing up with a twin sister who was stricken with a lifelong illness, and an older sister who was somewhat of a "miracle child," I felt ignored and overlooked a lot.

This is also an open apology for any miscommunication I might have had through the years where it seemed I didn't keep my word and inadvertently hurt people. This faulty communication of mine changed my life more than I wish to think about. So, to those who think negatively of me because of this, I am truly sorry. I never intended for certain things to happen the way they did. I am a woman of my word and I take responsibility for not being able to stop all the mistruths surrounding me and my career.

I should also note that *The Exorcist* was filmed many, many years ago. Events in this book are based on facts I remember, as well as facts provided by those close to me, and perhaps some events are in time a bit misconstrued, and perhaps some I just dreamed and think to be true. The purpose of this book is to simply be entertaining and if I have hurt anyone or anything on the way that was certainly not my intent and I apologize before the fact.

I heard someone ask Malcolm McDowell about what advice he would give an aspiring actor. Malcolm said, "You can only become an actor when you are so obsessed and you simply can't do anything else." He also admitted he wouldn't recommend anyone become an actor but, "if it's there and you must have it, for better or for worse, then take it! Go on the ride. Go on the journey!"

So, this is it. This is me, exorcising my demons. Thank you so much for coming along on my journey.

A Kid from Bayside

I blocked out many details of my childhood. I was never mistreated though. In fact, my sisters and I were all treated very well. We were never beaten or smacked around or locked up in the playhouse in the backyard--which was little but big enough for a small bed and a child's table. It's just, at a certain point, things became so painful for a while that I apparently just decided to not remember those years. There are, however, lots of parts of my life I do remember. And so my tale begins.

I was born in New York City, the city of bright lights, the city that never sleeps. I have two sisters; Denise, or Deni, and Marianne. Deni is two years older and the princess of the family. Before she was born, my parents tried and tried to have a baby. After a long time of failed attempts they began to consider adoption. And then, just like that, mom got pregnant and Deni was born. She was the "miracle baby," and she became Daddy's little princess.

When my parents decided to try their luck again, they got a two-for-one with Marianne and I coming along together.

So Cute

My parents always said I am a minute older because I pushed my twin aside, waved my hands, and the doctor picked me up first. They also said we didn't feel like waiting the full nine months, which is why we were born a month early via caesarean. We should have been Aquarians rather than Capricorns. We were so tiny, barely the size of small chickens. I was about four pounds and Marianne tipped the scales at three and a half pounds. We spent the first month of our lives inseparable. Literally. We were in an incubator.

I've been asked a lot throughout my life about what it's like to have a twin and it's hard for me to answer. I mean, it really *was* like having another "me" around. We looked the same, our parents dressed us the same. It may sound cliché but every time I looked at her, it really was like staring into a mirror.

My parents told us we used to speak "baby-talk" and apparently had real conversations nobody else could understand. We would stand facing each other and I would say, "da-da," and she'd say, "de-de." To anyone else around, it was apparently like watching two people communicate. Except, we were the only two who knew what was being said.

My father, William Dietz and a West Virginian by birth, sold advertising space. He created ads with a copy writer and hired models and photographers to shoot the print ads. Then his company would sell the whole package to magazines, newspapers or billboards. He worked in mid-town Manhattan, at a place called Studio Associates, with a lot of highly talented and brilliant photographers in those days. He helped to set up the shots of models selling appliances, drugs, cigarettes and just about anything you could hold or look at. The models were the most beautiful, most exquisite women I had ever seen. (My mother would drive me and my sisters to visit my dad's studio from time to time.) The models must have been paid by the day because come five o'clock at night, they were gone. So the photographers had to work fast. Every time I walked through there it was like playing dodge-ball, except with cameramen rushing back and forth between rooms--a seemingly infinite number of cameras and lenses slung over their shoulders. It was a really neat place to spend time and I was fascinated by the people who worked there. Occasionally, someone would politely scoot me out of the way when they needed to get by. I was fine with that as long as I was able to find a place to play.

They had the most wonderful makeup room in the studio--a magical place for a little girl who wanted to be an actress. In that room, drawers and dressers were filled with cosmetics and jewelry, and closets were stuffed with costumes and women's lingerie. My father would let me poke around and have fun whenever my mother brought us all to meet him there after work. My sisters would follow my mother around his office and I would play dress-up with the costumes and act out my own scenes. It was lovely because I didn't have to be myself.

7

I could be anyone I wanted to be. Sometimes I was Ingrid Bergman, giving a heartbreaking farewell to Humphrey Bogart for the last time while getting on a plane, leaving Paris. Sometimes I was Donna Reed, welcoming home and kissing my disheveled (imaginary) James Stewart. It really didn't matter who. The only thing that *did* matter was, in that room, I was an actress.

Beatrice and William aka Mom and Dad

My father came from a very poor family. I don't remember much about my grandfather, but I do recall my grandmother. She was a simple, quiet woman, from the old country. And she frightened me. I always felt like she had some pent-up anger. I swear I saw it in her face, like she could explode into a rage at any moment. But, being a woman of that generation, and European, I assumed she was very good at never showing her emotions. She also never measured food when she cooked. I always found this interesting. She would stick her whole hand into a bag of flour, right up to her forearm, grab a fistful of the stuff and throw it into a bowl. I remember the "poof" sound it made and a white cloud would rise up. I used to watch her while she did this from around the door to the kitchen, but I don't remember ever having a conversation with her. I heard from relatives she ended up in a mental hospital when she got older. For some reason, I got it into my head that people who cried ended up in a mental hospital. This is the reason I never cried as a child. When I was upset, I would go to my room and hide my head under a pillow so no one would hear me. I was afraid that if I did cry, I would never stop and people would look at me funny and they would send me to that crazy place, like my grandmother. So, I cried alone.

My father eventually changed jobs and worked for another agency in an old fire house on the east side in

Manhattan. This studio was on Thirty-Third Street and Third Avenue. Any time we went down to visit him at the office, we'd say were, "going down to 'Toity-Tood and Terd.'" None of us actually spoke with a Brooklyn accent, we just had fun trying to sound like that.

My mother, Beatrice Schoenbrod, was originally from Chicago. My grandmother had always encouraged my mother to act. And although she was never an actress herself, Grandma was a real "stage mom." The only problem with this was my mother wanted nothing to do with acting. She never saw herself as an actress but her mother was sure she had "the stuff," so she pushed my mom a lot. She ended up doing one play called, *He Who Got Slapped*, in which she played a ballerina. But, all my mom wanted to do with her life was to get married and have kids. She didn't have any dreams about acting on stage. She did attend Northwestern for a while to study drama and journalism, but when the money ran out and she was unable to finish school, she decided to settle down.

My mother once told me a story about how she taught my father to wear shoes. I always found this odd. "Who doesn't know how to wear shoes?" I'd asked her. She said it was because he was brought up in a small mining town and all the kids ran around in the dirt without shoes. My father grew up poor and I suppose his father was just as happy his son went barefoot. This way, he didn't have to spend much money on my dad's shoes. After all, going barefoot ensures your shoes won't wear out so fast. Anyway, my mother told my father, "A businessman always wears a shiny pair of shoes." To that, my dad would respond, "I know how to wear shoes. I am going to be someone very important someday." And he was.

Beatrice Schoenbrod

Needless to say, my mother was not impressed by his style when they first met. But ultimately, it wasn't my father's lack of a fashion sense that won her over. My father was quite the charmer, and it was the Dietz charm over which my mother swooned. She was smitten by him, so much so that she gladly gave up the stage to marry him. And that was the end of her brief acting career.

My mother always insisted my dad was very much a "family man." Very "hands-on." You know, changing diapers, helping with feedings, attending doctor appointments, reading stories before bedtime, etc. All I can remember is he spent a lot of hours working at the agency, both day and night. Of course, it *was* the 1950s and not too many fathers during that time were as intensely involved with raising a family as they are today. Many a father was seen as the head of household; the man worked all day and the wife cleaned the home and took care of the children. Then at night, when the father came home, the wife cooked dinner for the entire family. It wasn't like today where fathers, in general, are far more involved with their families and most wives work full-time jobs as well. It was different when I grew up.

No Longer Twins

Throughout our lives my sister Marianne and I have had a kind of psychic energy when big events happen. Like when I knew Marianne had her first child, I knew exactly when it happened. Unfortunately, tragedy struck one day and she and I were never truly identical again. We still shared the same face but something happened to Marianne that caused her to be different.

My mother had taken all of us to the beach one afternoon. It was a day like any other, which is to say there was nothing truly memorable about it, just a sunny day spent at the beach with my mom and sisters. We swam in the ocean, collected sea shells, and chased the horseshoe crabs back into the water. It wasn't until the next day when Marianne complained about not feeling well.

Dr. Jay Lowen, a podiatrist, and a close friend of my family, rushed over to the house after my parents had called him. They ended up taking Marianne to the hospital and Deni and I didn't get to see her for a very long time. How long exactly, I have no idea but it seemed like forever. Deni, being the oldest, had a feeling something was wrong, but I was too young to know what. I just know she spent a lot of time away from home in a hospital bed, far from her own bed, from her sister--the twin version of herself.

My parents had tried to reinforce Marianne was okay but after some time, I started to ask questions like, "What's wrong with Marianne? When is Marianne coming home?" My mother would tell me, "Marianne isn't feeling well, but she'll be home soon." This was the most I ever got from my parents. I never quite understood her illness until I got older. I didn't understand how someone who was identical to me in every way could get sick and yet somehow, I remained perfectly healthy. It just never felt fair to me that she ended up the way she did. And, out of respect for my sister's privacy (and because this book is my story and nobody else's), I have chosen not to name her illness here, but rather to describe what happened and how my family dealt with it.

When Marianne finally did come home, I went rushing over to the car to greet her. I was so happy to see her and even happier when I saw her grinning at me through the car window. It was as if my other half had finally come back to me. Then she opened the door to get out of the car and all of that happiness quickly disappeared.

Marianne collapsed straight to the ground. She tried to stand up but she didn't have any strength to support herself. It was the scariest thing I'd ever seen in my young life. She was pencil thin, like she hadn't eaten or drank for weeks. She had no muscles in her left leg from the knee down and it was much smaller than the right one. She looked so weak and frail, and I remember staring at her in horror as my parents jumped out of the car to help her up. And then my mother simply told me, "Marianne can't run and play now." At the time, I didn't understand "now" actually meant "forever."

Deni and the Twins

As we got a little older and started going to school, I never did anything Marianne couldn't do. When the kids at school would go outside at recess and play hopscotch, I didn't join them. When they ran out to the playground to swing or slide, I didn't run with them. I pretty much stayed in step with my twin sister. I just never wanted for her to feel left out. By then, I was old enough to understand that life had been unfair

15

to her so I guess I just wanted to make some things a little fairer if I could.

We should have been identical still, running together, jumping rope, having our secret conversations, playing on the playground with the other kids. It was weird because although we were brought up atheists, I did believe in God. I thought God was angry and bitter and it was his *job* to punish bad little girls. I searched my brain to remember what I had done that was so bad. I even wished I had been adopted because that way, I wouldn't have felt so responsible for my sister getting sick.

I began to think that God had decided Marianne would be the one who got sick and, for whatever reason, I was the one he needed to spare. This is when I really started to feel guilty. It just wasn't right. We were the same. We *are* the same--twins. We should be exactly alike. If Marianne got sick, then I should too. If we were the same, then how come we were suddenly so...different? I also felt maybe God had only made Marianne sick *first* and that, eventually, he would give me something too. Later on, perhaps, when I was older. Except, I never knew when I was going to get sick. I thought I would wake up one day and have to be taken to the hospital, just like Marianne. Or maybe I would be in class, learning math or science or something, and suddenly, boom--I'd be sick.

On the rare occasion I did go out and play with the other kids, I always felt like a piece of me was left behind. She was somehow...broken, and couldn't be fixed. I once asked a teacher who I really liked, "Why can't God fix Marianne?" He told me, "God can fix Marianne, he just hasn't been able to yet because there are so many other boys and girls who also need to be fixed. And when it's Marianne's turn, he'll fix her too."

Marianne, Deni and Me

At home my parents had decided to put me and my sisters in separate bedrooms. I don't remember at all why my parents decided we had to be separated. I assumed the great Dr. Jay had probably suggested it. After all, he was a doctor (and my dad's closest friend). Whenever he made a suggestion, my parents almost always ran with it.

So Deni got a big bedroom. My parents told me it had to be this way because Deni was the big sister. End of story. Made sense to me. My parents also decided, due to Marianne's condition, she also needed a big room. So she ended up getting the biggest bedroom, the same one she and I used to share. It was all pink--pink walls, pink bedspread, pink rugs.

When we still shared the room, Marianne kept a lot of shelves on her side that held her plaster and pottery animals. On my side, it was all horses. Horses have always represented an escape for me. I didn't have one of my own but I always thought if I did, I could get on my horse and ride away and never come back.

Once, while I was at a sleep-away horseback riding camp, I wrote a story about a little girl who never got any attention from her family. She was completely on her own, with no one to talk to. But, the girl's family owned horses and at night she would walk into the corral and talk to her favorite one. The horse was her best friend. She could tell him about anything, and he would listen patiently and sympathetically.

18

Then one night, after the little girl's parents yelled at her for doing something wrong, the girl ran out to the corral, let the horse out of the stable and rode away, never to be seen by her family again. Then, every time there was a full moon, the shadow of the little girl could be seen racing across the moon on her horse.

Holly Brown Ranch Horseback-Riding Camp

When Marianne and I shared the pink bedroom I used to be awakened by soft sobbing sounds in the other bed. I knew it was Marianne crying, but I didn't know what to do. So, I let her cry. I was too scared to even try to help her, to ask what was

19

wrong. I guess I just always felt that whatever problems I had going on in my life, they were nothing compared to her problems and therefore, I would have no idea how to fix them. But I always felt I *had* to figure out a way to fix them. I can't stand it when I don't know how to figure something out. To this day I cannot bear to hear another person in pain. I simply have to try to fix her/him.

Marianne's room also had a private bathroom attached to it. My mom told me it was important so she wouldn't have to walk far if she needed to use the bathroom in the middle of the night. So, this is how she got the pink room.

I was left with the third bedroom, which was the smallest. It wasn't quite a closet, but it also wasn't much bigger, either. There was enough space for my bed and my dresser, and there was a small closet for my clothes. It had a window to the right of the bed, out of which I could see our huge weeping willow tree. The window had sheer curtains on it. Nothing "frilly" though. In fact, nothing in my life was. I never played with dolls or fake stoves or had little tea parties. Even as a small child, I always found those kinds of things to be stupid and silly. Sure, I was a dreamer and I played make-believe quite a bit, but only in my mind. I loved being alone with my dreams and my imagination. I could be anyone or anything; I could whisk myself away from the pain and the heartrending sounds of sobbing without the assistance of a single toy.

My father had a hard time connecting with me on a personal level after Marianne got sick. I used to parade around in tiny bikinis just to try to get his attention. He would ask me, "What the heck are you doing?" and then make me go change.

I never remember him hugging me. I think deep down inside he felt Marianne's disability was his fault. To that, I have to say I feel similarly. He was very much a perfectionist and couldn't abide by anything less than so.

My mom started drinking at this time and hid her vodka under the sink. Occasionally she would take a nip or two (or three) after the sun went down. But she was a happy drunk. Sometimes too happy, I think. She also took diet pills provided to her by Dr. Jay Lowen. Well, they called them "diet pills" but they were actually speed. My sisters and I all knew to stay away when she went off the pills. Eventually, mom lost a ton of weight by doing it the natural way: Weight Watchers. She stopped drinking and taking pills--those items weren't on the Weight Watchers approved list.

There were other things that were different after Marianne came home. I noticed we weren't treated the same anymore, certainly not like twin sisters. Her needs always had to come first. It began to feel as if we were no longer equal. Of course, I didn't and don't expect sympathy; it's just how it was. It was always about Marianne's health and overall comfort, which was fine. In fact, that's how it should have been so I was happy to see she was cared for as much as she was. But, it would have been nice to be noticed from time to time. I began to think I had middle-child syndrome. I'm sure my acting out as a kid had a lot to do with this. After all, when a child doesn't get attention, s/he looks for *any* attention, even if it's negative. This acting-out manifested itself during one of Marianne's therapy sessions.

For a long time, Marianne wore an ugly leather brace on her bad leg, the kind with steel supports on both sides. Then when she was a little older, just out of grammar school, she received an operation on her leg that allowed her to not have to wear the brace anymore. After the operation, she needed physical therapy. One therapy session I recall vividly is one they did in the pool.

Because my father was always working, my mother ended up having to bring me with her whenever she took Marianne for therapy. Deni was old enough to stay home by herself so it was just the three of us. And, since there was nobody to watch me while Marianne did her therapy, they had me join them in the pool so they could keep an eye on me.

I was already in the water when Marianne was letting herself into the pool. There were other people swimming laps, taking lessons…it was a big pool, large enough for multiple activities, but we stayed close to the edge in our little area so as not to disturb the other swimmers.

I remember the therapist asked Marianne to try kicking her legs. He wanted her to start building her strength back up in her weakened leg. It seemed to take a long time and I started to get bored so I wandered off into the swim lanes. My mother called me back, saying I was getting in the way of the other swimmers. I didn't think I was in anyone's way so I just kept swimming around. When my mother yelled at me, I swam back toward them.

I felt embarrassed being yelled at in front of all those people. So I decided I would make her feel bad for yelling at me.

I began to fake my own drowning. I went under the water and thrashed my hands back and forth, pretending I couldn't swim. Suddenly, everybody started to swim toward me. I was kicking and screaming and was eventually pulled out by a man who'd been swimming in one of the lanes. As he pulled me out of the water and laid me down onto the cement, I started laughing. This didn't go over well at all.

My mother scolded me (I think a few other people who were there yelled at me too). She told me what I did was very dangerous, very selfish, and someone could have really gotten hurt. They made me sit outside the pool for the rest of the session. I had to sit in a chair in my wet bathing suit for what felt like an eternity. Nobody gave me a towel so I started to get really cold. But nobody cared. I deserved it. Throughout the

23

session, I caught my mom glare at me from time to time with a look of disappointment.

Doctor Asshole

Dr. Jay Lowen and I had a "strained" relationship, to put it lightly. My dislike for Dr. Jay was simply in response to his dislike for me. That is, his *passionate* dislike for me. Dr. Jay absolutely despised me. I'm pretty sure it was because I was everything my twin sister should've been, and would've been, if she hadn't gotten sick. Dr. Jay felt if anyone *should* have gotten sick, it should have been me. After all, according to Jay, I was a "juvenile delinquent." At least, that's what he would tell my parents. Granted, I may have shoplifted a time or two, talked back quite a bit, told my piano teacher to go to hell (boy did I get punished for that), but it was really petty adolescent stuff. I was never in any trouble with the police. I didn't have a record or anything.

The most trouble I ever got into was probably the time I got "locked in" at the Bronx Zoo. My friend Alix Kane and I met at a horseback riding Summer Camp. We would ride horses all day but at night we would sneak out of our dorm and visit the boys' bunk. We became really close friends after camp, although her mom never liked me. Alix was a real Jewish princess and her mother didn't like her hanging out with a hippie who had stupid dreams about being an actress. Alix wore

Cashmere sweaters and I wore black turtlenecks with lined eyes and white lipstick.

Anyway, we decided to meet up with a couple of the boys at the Bronx Zoo. We spent the entire day with the boys we'd met at camp. We weren't reckless or anything, but we lost track of time and managed to stay until after it had gotten dark outside. Our parents were frantic since they didn't know where we were. They had almost called the police when I called my parents to come pick us up. We claimed they'd locked up the zoo and we were trapped inside. To this day, I don't even know if it's even possible to be locked in at the zoo, but my parents bought it. They still yelled at us for being careless, but they never questioned the fact of whether or not the zoo was closed. They also didn't know we'd met a couple of boys there. I'm sure Jay would have had plenty of opinions to share about that.

When I was in my teens, around the time I started to become interested in acting, Jay would tell me, repeatedly, I was too ugly, too short, and I didn't have the figure (i.e. boobs) to be a successful actress. His opinion was, in order to be an actress, a woman had to be drop-dead gorgeous with giant boobs, beautiful hips and long, slender legs. At the time I was very small and only grew to be barely five-feet tall and, throughout much of my youth, very androgynous. Thanks to Jay, I never forgot that.

Another time while participating in Phys. Ed. class at school, I was goofing off by swinging on the gymnastic rings, when my hand slipped and I fell. I landed really awkwardly and jammed my finger into the hardwood floor of the gymnasium. It hurt like HELL. I couldn't recall any pain like it in my life until then. I saw stars as I rolled around the floor, until the teacher helped me up and raced me to the school nurse. The nurse took one look at my finger and immediately said it was broken, so she called my parents to come pick me up.

Dr. Jay told my parents he would take care of me so they brought me to his office instead of the hospital. However, when he looked at my finger, he said it wasn't broken. He said I probably just suffered a "deep bruise." All I could think was, *are you kidding me*? He'd barely looked at my finger before he was wrapping it up and told me to put some ice on it. To this day, I still have a crooked finger.

Now you're probably thinking, "Why didn't someone tell Jay to go fuck off?" Well you see, Jay was also somewhat of a hero in our house. And although he was only a podiatrist he knew his way around the hospital and Marianne got priority treatment. He undoubtedly saved her life so I guess my parents felt they owed it to him to believe every word that came out of his mouth. He was one of those men who knew everything about everything and was always right--a know-it-all. I couldn't stand it. Every time he opened his mouth it was as if he was beginning a speech about the dawn of mankind. Bottom line; he was a jerk, he didn't like me, and I didn't like him. Period. He may have saved Marianne's life, and he may have been a hero, but this didn't change the fact he was an asshole. Hey, sometimes heroes can be jerks too.

And not only can heroes be jerks, they can be liars and cheats as well. After my dad's death, my mother told me a little secret. She and Dr. Jay had an affair for many years and she also told me, ironically, my father had also cheated on my mother for many years. He slept with many of the models who thought they could get ahead by having sex with the guy who hired them. A casting couch for models, I guess. My mother said she had known about it all along, but when I asked her why she stayed with him for all those years, she said, "It was okay as long as he brought home the checks." I never knew if she was joking or not.

When I asked my mother what kept them together, all those years, she told me they had wanted to stay together for me and my sisters. They stayed together in order to keep some semblance of a family.

But then my mom told me Jay's wife, Augusta, found out about her and Jay. At that point, all hell threatened to break loose. Augusta had said to end the relationship or she would tell my Dad. Maybe psychically I suspected Jay was a cheat and that was another reason I had such disdain for him.

CHAPTER TWO

Off to Neverland

It's kind of ironic that, even though I spent part of my childhood living in Manhattan, I never saw a Broadway play until *after* we moved out of the city. We had moved to Long Island (or, Bayside, Queens, depending on whom you were talking to; richer people live in Long Island, the poorer people lived in Queens) when my sisters and I were still very young. One day, my mother decided to take us into the city to see *Peter Pan* with Mary Martin.

I was so excited. Until then, I had only enjoyed acting by myself, in the solace of my own bedroom. I was thrilled to know there were people out there who got to do it *on a stage*. I began acting out scenes from *Peter Pan* in my bedroom. I flew away to Never Never Land in my mind, jumping--no *flying*--off of my bed. Sometimes I even took my act outside, to the gargoyles.

My dad had brought home a pair of gargoyles he'd gotten from the library. He thought they would look great in our backyard. We had a stone driveway, a patio out back, and a rolling lawn that led to a steep drop overlooking the Long Island Parkway which surrounded the bay off the Long Island Sound. My dad put the Gargoyles at the bottom of the lawn and they "guarded" our yard. I used to sit on one of the gargoyles and "race" away to lands far, far away, until my mother would call me in for dinner. When I found out we were going to see *Peter Pan*, I hopped on one of the gargoyles and flew far, far away with Tinkerbelle and the Lost Boys. I felt like the characters from *Peter Pan* would have accepted me as one of their own.

As the days went by and the show date got closer, I would ask my mom, from time to time, if we were still going. She reassured me every time. "Yes, Eileen, we're *still* going." Not that I ever doubted my mother's intentions. Because by the time we moved to Bayside, I knew if my mother said we were doing something, we were doing it.

Unfortunately, on the day of the *Peter Pan* show, there was a blizzard outside; absolutely the worst possible conditions. Trees were shrouded in snow--their branches arching toward the ground. The streets were covered with snow and we didn't know if we would get the station wagon out of the driveway. My sisters and I began to think we wouldn't get to go. But, my mother had bought the tickets well in advance and we were going to see a show, no matter what.

Sometimes, but not often, my mother really showed some gumption. A courageous woman, she marched for civil rights along with Marianne and me in our baby carriages. She was also very politically active in our community. She was even a near-card-carrying Communist when it was very chic to be, before McCarthy and the Un-American Committee came along. Our neighbor was the sister of Jerome Robbins, the famous director and choreographer who was brought up before the committee. He gave names. But I digressed.

Mom was also a Girl Scout Leader. In fact, her troupe was the first black/white integrated Girl Scout troupe in the 1960s. She was what you would consider a "feminist." That is, when my father wasn't around.

More often than not, as soon as my dad came home from work, my mother was always quick to revert to her, "serve-the-man" ways. She catered to him a lot. She never seemed to retain the same feminist strength when he was around, always deferring to his opinion. Whether it was about what time we kids went to bed, what we watched on television or what my mom would cook for dinner on any given night, mom was certainly "master" of our little domain. Until dad showed up.

But, my dad was at work the day of the show so, after mom decided no snow storm was going to thwart our attempt to get into the city, she bundled us up in our snow suits and we all set out.

Our house was about a good mile and a half from the Long Island Railroad Station and driving, unfortunately, was not an option. This didn't matter to my mom. We had an old wooden sleigh--the long straight kind with the curved lip in the front--and my sisters and I took turns riding while my mother pulled us through the thick blinding snow. Thinking back now it probably wasn't the greatest idea, but we were determined--my mother most of all. We were going to make it to the show, through rain or shine (or blizzard, in our case).

As mom pulled us down the barren neighboring streets; I was sure people were watching us from their houses. It was a strange feeling, the thought of all those eyes on us as we made the trek through our winter wonderland. I thought for sure anyone who saw us forging through the tundra would think we were crazy. What mother would risk traipsing through such a storm with three little girls? My mother, that's who.

After the sleigh ride we ended up making it to the station in decent time. By then, my poor mother was worn out. I could tell. She tried not to show it as she tried to control the pace of her breathing, but I knew she was tired. Her face was soaked with sweat, strands of hair streaked over her forehead. And her cheeks, reddened and cracked by the cold, were far redder than ours. But, she quickly produced all of our tickets and we took the train into the city and made it to the theatre on time to see *Peter Pan.*

We had seats in the first balcony, first row. I watched in utter fascination as Peter Pan and Wendy met. Then she and her little brothers were whisked away to Never Never Land. They took me with them to meet the little Lost Boys and those awful pirates! I was simply amazed at what I was seeing. I remember thinking so vividly, if I had only jumped off the balcony onto the stage and landed on my feet, I would look around and I would be part of the play. I imagined myself flying around the stage with the rest of the cast. I was a star in a Broadway play. Everyone in the audience loved me! I wanted to become a performer just like them. What a magical life these people, these actors, must have!

Of course, I never did fall from the balcony. I just stayed in my seat, next to my mother and sisters, and enjoyed every single second of it. Afterward, we met my father for dinner at a nearby restaurant. By then, after the snow storm had beaten up New York for most of the day and even the night, the city was practically abandoned and we had our pick of where to eat.

On the way home in my dad's car, satisfied by a full stomach, I curled up in the back seat content and happy. I was still very young, but I knew someday I would be on a stage, somewhere, creating the same magic I had seen that afternoon.

I closed my eyes and slowly let the images of Peter Pan flying across the stage carry me off to sleep on the ride home.

Tomato Juice and a Jelly Donut: Breakfast of the Stars

It would be a bit of an understatement to say it came as a shock to me when, on the day I finally told my mother I wanted to be an actress, she simply looked at me and said, "If you are good, you can be an actress." Well what the hell does that mean? If I'm bad, I *can't* be an actress? How do I know if I'm good or bad? I was just a tomboy from Bayside. Marianne and I were in a print ad at a mere 6 months old, but I'd never acted in a commercial or anything. How did she know? Don't actors have to practice in order to get it right? Nobody is an expert the first time out. But my mom's words made me think if I wasn't good the first time, then I'd never be good. It was a tough thing to hear, and it was an idea that would haunt me for the rest of my life.

My father was even less shy about his feelings regarding my desire to be an actress. Actually, he was painfully blunt. Apparently, my mom had shared my aspirations with him before I had a chance to talk to him about it. He dismissed my idea as nothing more than a childhood fantasy and he told me the only way I could ever become an actress was if I slept my way to the top. Why would he say something like that?

Somehow, I got them to allow me to take acting classes at a renowned school in New York City: The Neighborhood Playhouse. For three hours every Saturday, I was in a different world. There were kids like me, aspiring young actors and actresses. It was Heaven.

My First Acting Job with Marianne at 6 Months Old

Unfortunately, and just like at school, I never really felt like I fit in with the rest of the kids. They were all very good-looking. The girls were tall and slender, many of them from wealthy families. Even at such a young age, many of the girls had already started to develop their curves. I was wondering if mine were ever going to show up. I felt different from everybody else so I kept to myself. I simply went to class, participated in the assignments and went home. I never really made friends with the other kids.

I also never told any of my friends where I was going on Saturday mornings. At the time I was sure they thought (as I did) that movie stars were special. We, on the other hand, were "normal" people, I thought. Famous people weren't like us. They were...*different,* somehow. Like they were born differently or made differently or came from a strange, magical place. I just knew I wanted to be like the rest of the actors on stage and on TV and in movies. But, I couldn't bear the thought of anyone destroying my one and only dream more than they already had.

So, every Saturday I would walk three quarters of a mile to the bus stop near my house in Bayside. Then I would catch a 20-minute bus ride to Flushing, Queens. Once I reached Flushing, I took a subway to Third Avenue and Fifty-Second Street. After I got off the subway, I bought a tomato juice and a jelly donut. After breakfast I would take a right, walk two blocks, another right, one more block, then I was there: Heaven. When I was in class, I was a professional actress. There was no limit to where my talents could take me, nobody holding me back but myself. Until then the only experience I'd had as an actress was in my tiny bedroom. Now I was acting out scenes along with other kids--other would-be actors. It was difficult and scary, but I just knew I was right where I was supposed to be. I *felt* it. I even spent hours in class practicing and perfecting my autograph since, naturally, I would eventually have to sign it over and over and over…

We did one play, toward the end of the year, called *Dark of the Moon*. I had so badly wanted to play the lead, but the teacher's pet ended up getting the part. This girl was gorgeous. Tall, thin, huge boobs (for her age). I was crushed. I ended up playing a smaller role as a member of the town.

When class was over, I would retrace my steps home. No longer a star in my own mind, I was once again the Little Dietz Twin. But it was okay. It was only a matter of time until I would realize my dream. In a way, it was already starting to come true.

I'd always wanted to audition for the High School of Performing Arts. It was a place I'd heard about in my school. However, the fear of failure started to dig its horrible ugly nails into my tomboyish skin and I became too afraid to even audition. I felt if I auditioned and I didn't get in, then I would never become an actress. After all, my mother had told me as much and I didn't know if I would be good. So I simply decided not to try. This way I wouldn't be rejected and I wouldn't end up getting hurt.

I also never auditioned because if I had, I knew it meant I would have had to spend a lot of time away from

Marianne. I wasn't prepared for that; I couldn't simply leave her behind. I know now it was just an excuse. It wasn't necessarily because we were twins. It was a self-appointed task to take care of her. As a twin it felt like whenever Marianne wasn't around, a part of me was missing. Going to the Neighborhood Playhouse had been easy because it was only Saturday mornings. The High School of Performing Arts was just like any other school, Monday through Friday. But it was in the city, far away from Bayside, and I just couldn't do it. Of course, this was also a great excuse to not risk failure.

Sometimes Parents Just Don't Understand

There was a book and two films that inspired my dream. And it should come as no surprise I didn't agree with popular opinion of either of these works.

All About Eve is a fascinating story about a young, aspiring actress named Eve who would do anything to be successful. Betty Davis was the star. Anne Baxter played Eve. The movie sets up Eve as the villain because she wants to destroy Betty Davis. She even tries to take away Davis' husband in the movie. Personally, I never thought of Eve as a villain. I just saw her as a girl who would stop at nothing to be an actress. I didn't see anything wrong with how she went about trying to become an actress. Well, maybe the fact she tried to steal Davis' husband was going a little too far, but I still admired her perseverance!

And then there was *Rosemary's Baby* where Rosemary's/Mia Farrow's husband, played by John Cassevates, makes a deal with the devil to turn him into a famous Broadway star as long as Rosemary births the Devil's baby. Again, I thought, *Hell, if it ain't murder, larceny, theft, no one had to sleep with anyone on a casting couch, and no one gets hurt, then why not?*

The book that pushed me on was called, *Marjorie Morningstar*. It was made into a movie, starring Natalie Wood and Gene Kelly. Marjorie Morgenstern (Wood), an aspiring actress, goes to Summer Stock and falls in love with the director of the company, Noel Airman (Kelly). By the end of the summer, Airman breaks off the relationship. She leaves the company, crushed and heartbroken, but she still wants to become an actress. Her parents tell her a family friend, a dentist, knows someone in the entertainment industry who can help her. But Marjorie adamantly wants no help. She would rather become a star on her own terms, or not at all. When I saw the movie, I thought, *What's wrong with her? I would take all the help I can get.*

It was a fascinating story to me and I marveled at how this young girl went about becoming an actress with no help from anyone. I thought it was a lovely story and hoped I would one day be able to accomplish the same.

Taking inspiration from Marjorie Morningstar, I began looking for Summer Stock companies all over the country. I didn't have any money for professional pictures so, with my little Kodak camera set up on a rickety old tripod in my bedroom (what the hell did I know about 8x10s?), I set the timer and posed while the camera snapped off shot after shot. I sent the photos to every theatre in the book. I knew it was a long shot but what did I have to lose? So, off the photos went and I waited.

It was only a few weeks since I'd mailed out the pictures when I got my first call from a Summer Stock director. He invited me to spend the entire summer working with the theatre. It was my first big break! I was so excited. To think, someone actually wanted to give me a chance. I believed this was all I needed to begin my journey toward becoming a professional actress. I raced down the stairs to tell my parents and unbelievably, they said, "No!"

My dad said the director probably wanted nothing more than to get into my pants. I pleaded with my parents to let me go. I tried to explain how much it meant for me to work professionally and it would help me secure work in other stage and theater productions. My dad's response was, "What you need to do is get an education." My mom agreed. Their opinion was, it's nice that acting is fun for me, but I need to go to school and get a degree so I would have something to "fall back on." I didn't see school as being necessary since I already knew what I wanted to do, which was to act.

Words can't describe how distressed I was. They both had said "no." I ran upstairs to my bedroom and pulled the pillow over my head and cried until I had no tears left. By this time I believed it was okay to cry as long as no one heard me (i.e. I wouldn't end up in that mental hospital).

Strangely, the negativity I received from my parents ended up becoming my source of motivation. All I wanted was to be an actress and never have to go back to my old life; the one where I had somewhat become the forgotten middle child-- the little Dietz girl who was full of crazy dreams.

Unconditional support would have been wonderful, and I don't believe I would've made the mistakes and choices I made in my life if I'd had it. But this negativity worked for me too because every time someone told me I couldn't do something, it made me that much more determined to do it. It made me feel not only that I *could* do it, but that I *would* do it.

College Girl

I decided if I had to go to college, I would go to Carnegie Mellon. They had a great drama department and many famous working people had studied there. Unfortunately, they didn't offer a Bachelor of Science or Arts degree--they only offered a Creative Arts degree--and my parents weren't going to send me off to a school that didn't provide me "something to fall back on," and would only encourage my dream. So my second pick was Northwestern since that's where my mother had gone to school. They also had a great drama department. They accepted me too! The problem with going to Northwestern was there was no room in the dorm and my mother had always preached about, "having the real college experience," so that didn't work out, either.

College, being just as expensive then as it is now (relatively speaking), I pleaded for my parents to give me the money to set me up in the city. They didn't so much as bite. I couldn't even get them to negotiate. So one Saturday afternoon, my parents sent me to take a test for a college scholarship. It was one of those tests with lots of questions followed by a series of check-boxes. I sat there and idly filled in the boxes until I finished. To my surprise, I ended up getting a scholarship to a New York state school and my parents shipped me off to Syracuse University. Deni ended up going to Wisconsin and Marianne went to Boston University.

I knew right away college wasn't for me. In fact, I like to say I went to college for five minutes. I didn't pledge to a sorority. I just busied myself by taking courses in theatre and the arts. I didn't really see myself staying for four years, graduating and becoming an accountant, business woman, or something. New York City was still calling me.

41

On the upside, Syracuse *did* have a fairly well-known drama department. And since I was going to college, I thought I might as well study acting. It might actually make school fun. But much like in high school and at the Neighborhood Playhouse, I was very shy and couldn't fit in.

The head of the drama department told me personally I would never become a successful actress. He always said, "Acting begins in the feet." I never knew what the hell that meant. It's probably why he never cast me in anything.

I did meet my good friend, Bonnie, while at Syracuse though. She wasn't an outsider like me, so it's strange how we clicked, but we did. Bonnie lived in the city with her single mother, which was unusual for the time since most kids' parents were still together. Bonnie wanted to be an actress too. She'd gotten a lot of parts while at Syracuse and, by most accounts, was far more successful than me in terms of being cast in school productions.

I didn't get any parts while I was at Syracuse but I did stick around long enough to perform in my first professional play. It was called *Job* (named after the biblical figure). Job was played by Los Angeles Law's, Richard Dysart. I'd finally met a real life professional actor! My part was small, but I didn't care. I had a blast and was relieved to have finally gotten a role in a show, and not just any show, but a professional company. It wouldn't be long, I thought, until I secured more roles in more shows.

Moving Out

Bonnie and I left Syracuse and moved to New York City. We lived in a fifth floor apartment on West Twenty-First Street, between Eighth and Ninth Avenues. During this time it was a very poor neighborhood and certainly not the safest of places. But we thought this was a good thing and nobody would rob our place; they'd probably go uptown and steal from someone who had more money, more things.

Our neighborhood was mostly Spanish and our neighbors were very friendly. They offered to keep an eye on our place for us while we were out. We were two single girls living on our own, so it was nice to know our neighbors were looking out for us.

If you're going to work as an actor, either in New York or in Los Angeles, live cheap. Don't starve yourself, just live within your means. Don't go buying yourself expensive things, eating out at restaurants and throwing dinner parties for all your friends. Don't buy yourself an expensive car. In fact, don't buy a car at all if you don't need one. When I first moved into the city, acting jobs rarely came with a hefty paycheck. That's reality. I had to go looking for other work. When you're new to the business, jobs and roles don't coming looking for you. You have to go out and find work yourself. It's a tough business and I just had to accept it and either persevere or find another career.

I also feel like there's this preconceived notion among many an aspiring actor that once they get their first acting gig, the money will take care of itself and everything else will just fall into place. Well guess what? Some roles pay and some don't. If they paid well, I could survive on the cash I'd made while I was looking for another role. Between acting gigs, Bonnie and I would take part-time work. One of those jobs was dancing at a club in the city. No, not *that* kind of dancing. We just danced on the bar and got paid to entertain. We never took our clothes off because it wasn't that kind of club and we weren't interested in dancing naked.

Summer Stock

I eventually resumed my quest for Summer Stock experience. To my delight, I received several offers from various companies, but in the end it was "JR," a theatre director from Michigan, who had lured me in by offering me leads in several plays. Leads!!! It felt like a dream come true. JR had sounded so passionate and sincere when he asked me to join his company of actors. So of course, I thanked him and said I would love to be part of his summer stock theatre. I couldn't wait to get there. Unfortunately, JR and his company were not all that they seemed.

I met everyone from the company as we all arrived in Michigan. They all seemed so nice and welcomed me with open arms. It was the first time I'd truly felt like I belonged. Nobody stared at me strangely or whispered behind my back. It immediately felt like I was part of a family.

Later the same evening, JR asked me to come and see him. When I entered his office he was sitting behind a huge desk. It was made of dark wood, had squared-off corners and was much bigger in sheer size than any of the desks I'd seen at the Eileen Ford agency or even my dad's agency.

JR asked me to sit down on the leather couch that rested against the wall, opposite his desk. Not knowing what we were going to talk about, I took a seat, folded my hands and waited for him to say something. He immediately began telling me how fabulous I was and how happy he was about my deciding to come to Kalamazoo. I sat quietly for the most part, trying to take it all in. I kept thinking, *Yes! Yes! He believes in me*!!! I never even once considered it odd how he'd never seen me act before and yet, here he was paying me all these compliments. Again, naiveté won the day and I totally drank his Kool-Aid.

After a few minutes of praising me, JR started looking at me kind of strangely as he talked about the various plays the company would be performing throughout the summer and the "plans" he had for me. His eyes had a very suggestive tone to them, almost like he had some very immediate plans for me--

plans that might not involve theater. It made me feel even more nervous when he got up from behind his desk and walked across the room toward me. He took a seat on the couch next to me and again stared at me with those eyes, even more suggestive than before. I didn't want to overreact so I just sat there on the couch, frozen. I could no longer hear what he was saying because all I could think about was when I was going to get out of the office. When was he going to finish talking? When would he stop staring at me like that? When??? He mentioned something about the color of my hair and he reached out to touch it. I flinched so violently he pulled his hand back quickly. His face appeared surprised at first, but he laughed it off, said something about how he wasn't going to bite, and continued to touch my hair. As naïve as I was, I knew something wasn't right by now.

Before I knew it, he started to unbutton my blouse. I was shaking. I felt his fingertips graze against my bare skin as he loosened one button after another, but I sat there--tried to ignore it, tried to imagine it wasn't happening. What else was I supposed to do? It was my first night in professional theatre. I was in shock! I began thinking about all the young actresses who'd probably sat on this very couch before me. I wondered how many had reacted the way I was reacting and how many of them simply let it happen.

Then, before any clothes came off, JR decided we needed to have some drinks. He said I seemed very tense and that a drink would help to loosen me up. He let go of my shirt, stood from the couch, and when he turned, he whacked his head against a bookshelf, nearly gouging his eye out. It bled pretty well and he yelled loud enough for his wife and half the company to hear. They came rushing into his office and found JR bleeding like a stuck pig while I sat there, confused, blouse half-open, hair a tousled mess. I couldn't have looked any worse. There was no excuse I could come up with. I was the new girl, just in town that afternoon. Who was going to believe a word I said anyway? Needless to say, I didn't get the lead in any play.

The first, and only, show I did was *Camelot*. I played a little boy who wants to be a knight at the round table. They stuck me in a period costume that included these horribly uncomfortable red tights. I was unhappy about the whole situation. It wasn't the role I had been promised. It wasn't even close.

I was so unhappy I started eating peanut butter every night after dinner. A LOT of peanut butter...I began spreading it on bread and eating sandwiches. But eventually I worked my way up to spooning the gooey stuff right out of the jar and directly into my mouth. I gained weight but I didn't care. With every performance, my poor little thighs grew bigger and bigger, expanding my little red tights. I felt like the whole audience was watching my legs jiggle and stretch these tiny red tights. When it was my turn to be on stage, I could only think about how long it would be until I was back off.

What really hurt me was how people still believed I was sleeping with JR. Granted, it sure as hell didn't look good when they found me half-undressed in his office, but I'd thought for sure they would forget about it. I tried so hard to not let it affect me. I knew what they thought wasn't true, and that's all that really mattered, but it was difficult to ignore the stares, the whispers. I was starting to regret I'd ever come to the Barn Theatre.

JR ended up rooming me with this very sweet girl who turned out to be a lesbian. She was the assistant stage manager. She was small and very thin. She was actually quite androgynous, much like me; no boobs, short, cropped blonde hair, boyish. She was a very nice girl though and I remember nobody made any effort to talk to her except for me. I suppose that's why I felt connected to her. Until then, I'd spent most of my young life being overlooked by most of my family. We were kind of like the two outcasts. So, we had to stick together.

She thought it was so neat that I got to go out on stage every night. Meanwhile, I was jealous she didn't have to be on stage at all. In any case, she didn't have to wear those embarrassing red tights like I did. She was always there on stage though, as the assistant stage manager, watching every show, and after every performance, she'd tell me how she thought I did such a great job. For the first time, it was nice to hear such positive feedback from someone.

She also saw how lonely I was and how the rest of the cast had been treating me and felt really bad. She would try to cheer me up by saying things like, "you're a better person than them…you're a better actress…you'll be on to bigger and better things in no time…" Being a straight girl, I couldn't imagine how tough it must have been to be the only gay person at the theatre. I didn't really know how to respond. But then, it seemed I really didn't have to as she was always the one trying to cheer me up.

We talked one night about what our plans were prior to coming to Summer Stock and what made us choose the Barn Theatre. She'd wanted to learn more about the actual production of a play and wasn't interested in being an actress. I told her how I'd wanted to be an actress for many years, about Neighborhood Playhouse, about all the leads JR had promised me. I also told her how everybody thought I was sleeping with him. She felt bad for me. That's when she made her move.

She started to lay me down on the bed. I'd never been with a girl before so I was extremely nervous. At first, I thought I would just go with it. I was so lonely and sad and she was the first person who'd shown any interest in me, the first person

49

who cared, who thought of me as something other than the director's mistress. But in the end, I couldn't do it. I gently pushed her away and told her I didn't like her like *that*. I felt bad, but I'm just not into girls. Not now and not then. She understood though and we left it at that. Then I turned and noticed the peephole in the wall. Like a scene out of *Porky's*, JR had been spying on us the whole time.

I got fired shortly after. I was thrown out of my room, banished from the company. Unfortunately, my bus didn't leave until the next day and I had no place to sleep, but luckily, there was a set on stage that had a bed on it. So, my last night with the company, I slept alone on a fake bed with a fake mattress in a fake bedroom. Funny how it never occurred to me back then--I finally had my first on-stage lead. I was the star in my own one-act play. "Come see Eileen Dietz! One night only!" Despite all the stories about spirits haunting an empty theatre, I still managed to sleep through the night.

On the long bus ride back to New York, I thought about what I would tell everyone at home. I had been so proud, so excited. I was going to be a star. And yet, I felt like a complete failure. I was coming back to New York early, my tail between my legs and my pride unbelievably fractured. My dream had been crushed by the false assumptions and stares of the company members.

Or had it?

After all, none of it mattered as I looked down at my hand and saw my Union Equity Card. Regardless of what the company thought, I was a professional actress. Damn them all.

As far as the JR story, I did report him to the Actor's Equity when I returned to New York. Unfortunately, sexual harassment wasn't handled like it is these days and I'm pretty sure they just swept it under the carpet. I often wonder if JR is still pestering little girls with dreams of making it big.

Breaking Up the Band

Because we were actors we always wanted to make sure we looked our best. This is also where our neighbors proved very helpful. Whenever we left the apartment, knew we looked good if our neighbors whistled. If they didn't whistle, we would run back upstairs and change. We always made sure they whistled before we left, especially when we were going dancing or going to an audition.

The club where we danced belonged to Monty Rock III. This was before he'd appeared on *Merv Griffin*, *The Tonight Show*, and then later on, in Las Vegas. He was a hairdresser at the time, but his passion was running his club on the side. He was just like Bonnie and me; just trying to pay the rent so he could afford to keep the club open. It was tremendously exciting and fun working there. We wore white go-go boots and hip-huggers with short tops and danced to rock and roll songs like the "Mashed Potato". Monty Rock sang "On Broadway" (among other songs) and to this day, whenever I hear the song, I think of Bonnie and my adventures at his club.

Trying to Look My Best, Backstage at a Play

Monty lives in Vegas now and writes a gossip column for a paper *Gaming Today*, which is also an information column about what shows are playing in Vegas and why people should go and see them. He is also a practicing minister and marries people. It's amazing to me to see the paths certain peoples' lives have taken.

Bonnie and I also worked with a group called Plays For Living. It's still around today. They use live theater as a medium to explore social issues that are often difficult to talk about. Issues like race, sex, rape, drugs, etc. They're used as teaching tools designed to help children cope in these situations. We would often travel to private girls' schools as well as clubs for poorer kids. It was a great experience, and it paid some money too; but Bonnie and I were just happy to be working. We were a couple of single girls who, aside from acting, just wanted to live in the city, have freedom and have fun. I was the proverbial Clyde to her Bonnie. Unfortunately, Bonnie and Clyde came to a screeching stop.

Bonnie met a man and soon she wasn't around very much. We were still living together, but I quickly found myself looking for work alone as she spent more and more time with her boyfriend. I no longer had my buddy with me when I went out for auditions. Eventually, she stopped dancing at the club, too. When that happened, I knew it was only a matter of time.

Her boyfriend proposed not long after they began dating and she moved out. Once again, I found myself alone. My parents suggested I move back home, but I just couldn't live under their roof, again. I was free and owed nobody anything. I gave up the little apartment on Twenty-First Street and moved uptown to West Seventy-Third, off of Broadway. Even if I was broke and living job to job, I still had my own place. I was still on my way to becoming an actress, no matter what.

Smells Like Chocolate

I got an offer to do a children's theatre series for public TV, recreating the lives of famous, historic people (Thomas Edison, Ben Franklin, et al) when they were kids. I played the sisters or friends of these famous people. It was an hour-long program and the funny thing is, they weren't editing tape, so everything had to be done in one take. This kind of make-or-break filming served up quite a few lessons in learning your lines and shooting on time. I also got to meet my second famous person, Jean Stapleton of *Archie* fame. She played the teachers and Moms. What a sweetheart she was.

There was one actor, a very nice old man. He was always the first one to show up on set, always had snacks for the other actors. He especially treated the actresses nicely; told us how beautiful we were, how we were all going to be big stars one day. He gave us all tons of confidence. Unfortunately, he was also *very* forgetful.

Children's Theatre with Jean Stapelton in Hershey, PA

Children's Show in Hershey, PA

I remember any time he was on camera, the entire cast held their collective breath, hoping he would make it through his part without a hitch. Otherwise, we had to start the entire show over. He was usually good with his lines; he just had trouble learning his cues. So there was always this deafening silence any time he was on. Some actors even placed bets on whether or not the old man was going to nail it or if we were going to have to start all over.

It was shot in Hershey, Pennsylvania, and the set really did smell like chocolate. Every day.

An Early Lesson in Line-Delivery

One of the first real jobs I ever had was *The Doctors*. I only had one line on the whole show, but it was yet another valuable learning experience. I found out it's just as difficult to perform a single line of dialogue as it is to deliver multiple lines. In fact, sometimes it's even harder. I found myself repeating the one line, over and over in my head. It got to the point where I had focused so hard on *not* forgetting the line that I was overly nervous when we filmed the scene.

I could feel my whole body shaking as we shot. I waited tensely for my big moment. When it came, I delivered the line and they moved on. I immediately thought, *What the hell was I so worried about?* I was working on a Soap Opera. And who cared if it was only one line? I was on TV.

CHAPTER THREE

Unemployed

One of the coolest things about being an actress, and this might sound contradictory, is collecting unemployment.

In New York City, unemployment was based on the number of weeks worked so we always prayed a job would last through a Friday and the following Monday because, even though it was only two days, Friday and Monday counted for two weeks. When I accumulated enough hours, I would simply collect unemployment to stay afloat between jobs. My expenses were so low I was able to live off unemployment. We didn't have credit cards so we didn't have debt. I would head down to the unemployment office, collect my cash (they didn't mail checks in those days) and go home.

The cool part is I had to mention my profession on the unemployment application. So for me, it would say, "Actress." Even the government knew I was a professional actress!

Unfortunately, my parents didn't find this to be very cool, my dad especially. He still harped on me to get a job that included a Monday through Friday schedule. He didn't understand I was having too much fun pretending to be other people. It didn't matter to me that I wasn't raking in the cash. I knew what my limits were and I was conscious about living within my means. In fact, I'd have to say I was really good with my money. But, my dad never saw things the way I did. He said it was time for me to meet his friend, Eileen.

Eileen Ford

My father, ever the constant destroyer of dreams, told me I had to give up on, "the acting thing." I tried to explain to him how I really was getting onto films and on TV. By then I'd already done a couple of soaps: *The Doctors* and *Love of Life*, and I'd done some stage work. I'd made a little money but of course, my dad would say I wasn't making enough money. I would tell him I also took part-time jobs to supplement my income and I was "getting by". "'Getting by' is not earning a living," he told me. He was still so hell-bent against me becoming an actress that he set up a meeting with The Eileen Ford Agency, only the biggest modeling agency in town.

One sunny afternoon, and in an effort to appease my father, I walked over to the Eileen Ford Agency in Manhattan. My father told me he thought it would be a good idea to talk to someone like Eileen because she'd been in the business for a long time and knew what it took to get somewhere in the industry. He said I would benefit by getting some advice from her. I am sure my father thought I would be so depressed after talking to her that I would give up my crazy dreams. I am equally sure he told Eileen to really hammer it in to me, just how hard the business could be.

The Agency had an office like I'd never seen before; wall-to-wall carpeting, vivid colors, pictures of gorgeous models hanging on all the walls. In the center of the room was a giant reception desk, behind which sat a young, beautiful woman who could have been a model herself. She asked me to have a seat; Ms. Ford would be with me in a minute.

I remember sitting on a couch, watching all these beautiful, tall, curvy women walking by. I thought, *I look nothing like these women. Why am I here? I don't want to be a model I want to be an actress. I don't belong here.* I found myself staring up at these people, all five-foot-two of me.

After a few minutes Eileen finally came out and sat down next to me. She extended her hand and introduced herself. I took her hand in mine. It was the softest, most elegant hand I'd ever shaken. She was very pretty and smelled of a wonderful perfume. She said it was a pleasure to meet me. I guess I was a bit in awe of her because I don't really remember saying anything back. I mean, it was Eileen Ford! The woman was basically an institution.

After we exchanged pleasantries, Eileen was all business. She mainly spoke and I mainly listened. She gave me this very patronizing look and told me, albeit very nicely, it was very hard to be a model, and even harder to be an actress. She pointed at all the women walking by and mentioned even for these women, the gorgeous specimens walking by, it would be hard for them to be successful in the modeling business. Models had to look a certain way. And, she continued, the same went for actresses. Actresses had to be beautiful, striking; people the audience would want to see on a big screen. Movie studios didn't hire ordinary-looking people, she told me.

"Modeling" in Front of my Dad's Rolls Royce

Now Eileen never outright told me, "you'll never be a successful actress," but for the most part she kindly dismissed any notions I had of breaking into the business. I assumed

60

she'd done what my father asked, which was to reiterate what he'd already told me. I then began to realize there might have been a conspiracy between Eileen and my father.

My main take-away from the meeting with Eileen Ford was this: Actresses look like Marilyn Monroe or Jayne Mansfield or even Audrey Hepburn. They don't look like me. So I walked out of the agency and thought, *To hell with my dad! To hell with Eileen! What do they know? They work with models. I'm going to be an actress!* None of what she said mattered to me. I knew what I wanted and I would eventually figure out how to get it.

Teenage Gang Debs

Not long after my meeting with Eileen Ford, and with a fresh supply of motivation, I hit the Actor's Equity office and checked for casting notices, postings, and auditions. I did this a lot in those days. I had also finally learned how to take some decent headshots so I'd drop those off from time to time. The practice of getting an acting job became my nine-to-five.

Other than casting notices at the Actors Equity Union office, publications like *Dramalogue* or *Backstage West* were always good sources for work. It was in Backstage West where I'd seen a notice for a film called *Teenage Gang Debs*.

Teenage Gang Debs is an independent teen-exploitation film, shot in Queens. The ad I found said they were looking for actors to play rival gangs fighting over turf. Teen-exploitation films were very popular in those days. They were typically shot in black-and-white and were known to have outstanding soundtracks. *Debs* was no exception. A lot of these films were shot in the south too, so the fact they were shooting one in Queens was pretty cool.

The film stars Diane Conti, who plays a bad girl from Manhattan. She gets in with the leader of a Brooklyn gang, only to get him killed in a fight with a rival gang. She then starts dating the new lead guy and begins her plan to take down the gang, one by one.

I played Ellie, girlfriend of a guy named, Piggie. Piggie, unfortunately, dies in a knife fight so I had this big crying scene. It was the first time I'd ever had to cry on camera. I remember the day we shot it. The director, Sande Johnsen, came to me and asked, "Have you done a scene like this before?" Meaning: have you cried on cue before? I lied and said, "Yes." It was a dramatic scene, one of my first, and I thought if he knew I had never cried on camera before, he might rewrite the scene for another actress.

We shot the scene in a couple takes. Before each one, I would turn away from the rest of the cast and crew and rub my eyes until they burned. Then, when we did the take, my eyes were so irritated and dry, they naturally welled up: Tears! Sande was satisfied with the scene and that meant a lot to me because along with being a great guy and a great director, he was also gorgeous.

I had a major crush on Sande. I tried not to let it show, but I found myself staring at him from time to time. He just exuded this confidence, as directors tend to have. But, I kept my unrequited love to myself. I didn't want to do or say anything that would jeopardize my role in the film. Nor did I want to visit a "casting couch" even though I was already cast.

I also made a life-long friend while making *Debs*. Robin Nolan, who lived down on the East side at the time we made the movie, was a wonderful person. She and I hit it off right away, which was strange since she was totally a "downtown" girl.

"Uptown" actors were looked at as being more commercially-focused whereas "downtown" actors were more into the arts. If you wanted to act for the money only, you went uptown. If you wanted to do it for the art, you went downtown. I did both. When I was uptown, I wore short skirts and white go-go boots. Downtown, I wore tattered jeans, dark makeup and my hair down. I looked like a hippie when I was downtown. People uptown would ask me, "Why do you want to go down into the East Village?" People downtown would ask, "Why do you want to sell out and go uptown?" Somehow, I managed to balance myself between the two "towns."

Robin was much more grounded than I. In fact, she taught me a lot about spirituality. Not in the sense of

Catholicism or Christianity. Robin was into more "alternative" forms of spirituality. She burned a lot of incense, practiced meditation, and didn't eat meat, that sort of thing. She even knew which incense to burn, when to burn it and why.

Being brought up atheist I didn't really understand religion. I didn't understand spirituality either, but Robin showed me what it meant to her. I guess it was her outgoing and accessible personality that helped me to see certain things differently. Even after filming wrapped, we continued our friendship for many years. Even if it had been a year or so since we'd last spoken to each other, we always managed to pick right up where we'd left off.

It really crushed me when, just before the millennium, she died of cancer. She and her husband had moved out to Los Angeles about three years before she passed away. We had remained in touch even before she moved out west, so I was excited when she came to live out here.

Robin had this couch in her house that was right out of a therapist's office. It sat against the wall in their living room and had a little chaise extension. I would lie on it and we would just talk about whatever was going on in our lives. I remember she had been going through some issues with her husband at the time. He wasn't the nicest of men, for sure. But, through it all she remained one of the strongest people I've ever met, even as the cancer ate away at her body. Sometimes I feel like I should have been the one listening to her problems, helping her deal and cope with her issues; not selfishly blabbering on about what was happening in my life. But that's who she was. She had a heart of gold and her strength was truly an inspiration to me. I've never known another person like Robin in my life and I don't expect I ever will. She was a very special friend and one who I miss dearly.

Many years after we filmed *Teenage Gang Debs*, my husband was channel-surfing late one night and happened to catch a special about 1960's exploitation films called, *Reel Wild Cinema*. Being a film nerd in his own right, he stayed up to watch the entire show. While we were having breakfast the following morning, he turned to me and asked, "Did you do a movie where you wore a bouffant hairdo and white go-go boots?" Sheepishly, I said, "Yes." He then proceeded to tell me about this film called *Teenage Gang Debs*, specifically about a section of the film that was featured the night before during a program hosted by Sandra Bernhard. He mentioned one of the characters, Ellie, bore a striking resemblance to a younger me. I quickly fessed up and told him it was my feature film debut.

And here's another reason why I love him so much: he had the presence of mind to write down the information on how and where to buy the movies featured during the show. So we mailed for the DVD and a t-shirt! What fun to watch this film so many years later!

Acid Root Beer

I was "unwillingly" stoned while working on a film with Natalie Wood. It was during the New York City taxi strike so I wasn't able to get home one night. Sure, I could have taken the subway or a bus, but it was about midnight and the subway was not a safe place for a single woman. I also didn't feel like hopping on a bus so I shacked up at a friend's house (at least, I *thought* she was a friend).

My friend was having some people over and we were all having a good time until another one of my "friends" decided to put acid in my root beer when I wasn't looking. And I had to work the next day on the Natalie Wood film. I only had one line or so, but I still had to go and perform. Unfortunately, since I wasn't aware my root beer had been tampered with, I ended up going to work stoned on acid.

I used to believe the mind is stronger than any drug. I would think, if I ever found myself having to work while I was high, stoned or drunk, I'd be just fine. Turns out I was wrong. At the time it felt right, and working seemed like so much fun, even while slightly tripping. Everyone on the set looked so *odd*. I remember thinking it was strange how they were all 'making believe' and 'pretending' to be other people, in character and in costume. At one point I had to make my way to wardrobe. Natalie was in there. She was wearing this thick fur coat. I thought she was some kind of huge animal. Embarrassed, I turned and ran out of the room. I did come back later and tried on the coat and it fit perfectly.

I haven't had root beer since that day.

After the acid-root beer incident, one would think that if faced with the choice, I'd never mess around with drugs, either before working on a film or going to an audition, again. Sadly, it took one more horrible experience for me to finally realize drugs and performing don't mix well.

Just Say 'No' to Drugs!

I was up for a role in the Sandy Dennis movie, *Up the Down Staircase* and I decided to stop by a friend's apartment the night before the audition. It was late and I'd been depressed all day but she was having some people over and I thought, *screw this*, and decided I could use some company. Unfortunately, I never made it to the audition.

I had a few drinks soon after I arrived. The alcohol only made me *more* depressed and I basically just moped around the place. Somebody noticed I was feeling a little blue and asked me if I wanted to do some cocaine. He told me it would really help with my depression. "All you do is snort it," he told me. I'd never tried the stuff before in my life. I knew what it was though. The way he described it, it seemed interesting and sounded promising so I figured, *why not?*

So I snorted a little. I didn't notice anything. I actually didn't feel any different at all. I certainly didn't feel any worse, but I also didn't feel any better. So he told me to try a little more, and I did.

At some point during the night I blacked out, so I have very little memory of what happened. What knowledge I do have of what happened afterward is based purely on what my friends told me. They told me at first, I passed out. Then I turned blue. Then it appeared I'd stopped breathing. That's when they called a doctor.

After they tried to explain what had happened, the doctor initially didn't want anything to do with it. So he basically told my friends, "Good luck with the girl who blacked out. Hope she doesn't die," and hung up. Well, he must have had a change of heart because eventually he came to the house. I was still unconscious. For how long, I don't know. But he shot up my arm with caffeine and adrenaline and brought me back.

I say, "brought me back" because I'm positive I was not in the house at the time. I'm not exactly sure where I was. All I can tell you is what I saw: some of the most gorgeous, gold-colored figures beckoning me to come with them. I remember seeing them on a beach. They were playing in the surf, splashing and having fun with each other. They kept waving me over to them. "Come on, Eileen! Come with us," they were saying. I was ready to go with them too. I was more than happy to go be with the gold people, having fun on the beach. They would have welcomed me and treated me as one of their own. It was just the kind of thing to cure me of my depression.

Then I felt someone slapping my face. It was the doctor reviving me. The gold people suddenly disappeared and their world faded to black as I woke up. I was again back in the house, lying on the floor, cocaine dust on my nose and finger tips. I remember feeling so awful. I couldn't believe I'd done that. It came as an even bigger shock when the doctor revealed to me I hadn't actually snorted cocaine, I'd snorted heroin.

To this day I wonder how close to death I'd come. I believe I had an "out of body experience" and was very close to dying. I never made the audition due to my being messed up.

The doctor who saved my life was not only a physician, he was also a hypnotist. He invited me to come to his office and talk about how hypnosis might help with my feelings of depression. He said he wanted to help me figure out why I was so depressed. He seemed to be very concerned and genuine in his desire to help so I accepted his offer.

Now for those who don't know, the basic concept of hypnosis is that you will not do in real life what you will not do under hypnosis. At least, this is what I've been told. Anyway, I visited him at his office once and after he put me under, I remember he started asking me to take my clothes off--Oh god, I've been in this situation before: Man invites young actress to his office…tries to get her to remove her clothes…

I never took my clothes off and ended up running out of the office. I decided then and there hypnosis wasn't for me. I also decided I would never drink or get stoned before an audition. It was the only audition I've ever missed in my life.

David Holzman's Diary

One of my favorite films, *David Holzman's Diary*, was never released theatrically, and only recently on DVD and now on blu-ray. The film is used as a teaching tool in film schools across the country. It was also chosen for preservation in the National Film Registry. It was the first film to break the "forth wall," in that the main character speaks directly to the audience through the camera.

The movie is about a filmmaker named David Holzman, played expertly by L.M. Kit Carson, who decides he wants to put his whole life on film. As he follows himself around with his camera, he also starts following his girlfriend, Penny. After all, Penny is part of his life and he wants his whole life to be in the film. I played Penny.

One day we were shooting the scene where David is filming Penny while she sleeps. I get into position on the bed and start pretending to sleep. Kit has his camera and he's ready to start narrating, as he does throughout the film. But, before we start rolling, the director, Jim McBride, decides my character had to sleep nude.

Per the script, I had always assumed Penny would at least be wearing a t-shirt and underwear during this scene. I hadn't read anything about nudity. So naturally, all the red flags went up. I thought, *Wait a minute. I'm not going to be nude. I didn't know about this.* I didn't care about being nude. I was much more worried about any repercussions. *Would serious actors really do nudity?* I thought. Then I decided in all likelihood, nobody would ever see this movie. I also didn't want to stall the film, hemming and hawing over whether or not I wanted to be seen naked, so we shot the scene with me nude.

The scene pretty much happens like this: The camera pans across a dimly-lit bedroom, eventually focusing on a nude Penny lying on the bed. David is talking about Penny while she sleeps. Penny rolls over several times as her sleep has become disturbed by David's narration. Then she opens her eyes and sees David with his camera pointed at her. I get up, run across the room, yell at him to turn it off and I try to break the camera. The scene then goes black from there.

It was all done very quickly, actually. Plus, the room was very dark so I didn't think much of it afterward. Until one day…I was on the bus riding down Fifth Avenue, looking at *Life Magazine* when I came to an article about *David Holzman's Diary*. Included with the article was a still from the movie. The figure in the picture was mostly shadowy and silhouetted but you could easily tell I was nude. I immediately began to think about what my parents might say. What would my father say!!! Lucky for me they didn't put my name under the picture and even luckier, they didn't see the magazine and it never came up in conversation. Somehow, I'd escaped my only nude scene without much public or any private embarrassment.

David Holzman's Diary

CHAPTER FOUR

Using my Summer Stock experience, I managed to find work with another theatre company. I worked on two plays--*The Impossible Years* and *Barefoot in the Park*--at the Mount Gretna Playhouse in Pennsylvania. The director was a kind, old man named Charles Coughlin who couldn't hear very well. It was kind of funny because we would do a whole run through of the play and all he would say was, "Louder, louder!"

The woman who played the mother in *Barefoot* had a very bad drinking problem and she was only able to work on the play under the condition she not drink during the play's run. Everything was fine in the beginning. She'd honored her end of the deal...until she began appearing drunk on stage. And it wasn't like she was trying to hide it either. She'd slur line after line, she would stumble across the stage, and she nearly tripped over her own feet a couple times. The strange part is, none of us ever smelled alcohol on her. Nor did we see any evidence like empty cans or bottles of alcohol. We were befuddled. But one day, soon after the play's run was over, we found the culprit--a dozen empty cough syrup bottles. Where there's a will there's a way, I suppose.

Foul

Every actor knows that sometimes when you audition for the role, you don't get it. Hey, it happens. In fact, it happens a lot. And if you're an aspiring actor, you better get used to it. Personally, I've never taken rejection well. I once worked for a restaurant, between acting jobs, that required me to stand outside wearing a red cape, and hand out fliers. It wasn't the greatest costume I've ever worn, and probably not the worst, but needless to say, it was a little embarrassing. To top it off, people weren't accepting my fliers. At first it wasn't a big deal, but after a while it started to get frustrating, even a bit offensive. They would walk by, I'd stick my hand out, say something nice and inviting about the restaurant, and they would purposely walk *around* my outstretched hand. It's a free flier, people! Just take it and throw it away when you turn the corner! After about an hour of that, I threw the rest of the fliers in the garbage and turned in my cape. It was my last day on the job. I think it was also my first.

So, as with most things in life, rejection is also a huge part of acting. You're not going to get most of the roles you audition for. Each audition is like a job interview. You audition and then they thank you for your time. If you don't get the job, it likely had nothing to do with your audition. It might be you're too small, or you don't look tough enough, or they want someone with lighter hair. Essentially, you never know for sure why, but it's never anything personal.

An acting teacher once told me, "If you're absolutely sure you gave a great performance at the audition, then you have nothing to feel sorry about." For the most part, the casting director already has a certain look s/he is trying to find. If you don't have the "look," then you're destined not to get the part. But at least you know the rejection wasn't based on your performance. It's only a small consolation, but in my case, it was enough to keep me from getting discouraged.

So, sometimes you auditioned for the part and you didn't get it. Big deal. Life goes on. However, strangely enough, when I auditioned for a PBS special, I tried out for two roles, but ended up getting three.

Foul was a special about the ill effects of pollution. PBS had invited a group of off-Broadway playwrights to contribute a short play. Each commenting on various aspects of pollution and what it means to the future of the environment. Playwrights like Leonard Melfi and Israel Horovitz offered short plays. Being familiar with Melfi, Horovitz, and many of the playwrights who were involved, I wanted in.

Melfi contributed a piece about a hippie couple trying to have a baby. At the time I had long straight blonde hair, and was as much a hippie in real life as the one I would later play on

PBS. I decided I was perfect for the part.

For a different play, they wanted someone who could perform the part of a twelve-year old girl. I remember thinking, *I can do this*. After all, my tiny, androgynous frame had allowed me to believe as much. So when I told them I wanted to audition for both roles, they were fine with me auditioning for the hippie, but they didn't feel I was right for the part of the little girl. I'm sure all they saw was a short, thin, young woman with long blonde hair. As a rule, it's *very* bad to say you can do something if you can't do it. And I don't like to make promises I can't keep. But in this case, I was sure I could pull it off.

As I waited for my audition, I started planning it all out in my head. I would do the audition for Melfi's play and deliver my best "hippie" performance. Then, I would run to the bathroom, braid my hair, change into a dress, put on some stockings, come back out and audition for the part of the little girl. Who knows, maybe they wouldn't even recognize me.

So I auditioned for both parts, and once again, my slender frame turned out to be an asset. They wanted me for the part of the pregnant hippie as well as for the part of the little girl and even for a third role.

Sam Waterston, of *Law and Order: SVU*, and I worked on Melfi's *Puck, Puck, Puck*. It's about two hippies who never eat meat, only chicken. Chicken for breakfast, lunch and dinner. We move to a farmhouse in the woods to get away from the toxic city. My character is pregnant and both she and Sam, who played my husband, are getting ready to have the baby. Throughout the pregnancy they never eat red meat because cows and pigs were being manipulated with and contaminated by growth hormones and other pollutants in the environment. The only meat people could safely eat was chicken because there weren't any added hormones in poultry.

In the play our main concern is that our baby be born without any health defects. However, by the end of the play, and after eating nothing but chicken, my character ends up giving birth to a chicken egg. It was brilliant.

After *Puck, Puck, Puck,* I had to change into my little girl's outfit in order to do a play called *Trees,* with Phil Bruns. The same Phil Bruns of *Mary Hartman, Mary Hartman* fame. Phil and I played a father and daughter looking for a Christmas tree on Christmas Eve. The trees, a big tree and a little tree, were played by two black actors. The big tree was the father and the little tree was the son. So the two trees see me and Phil walking around the tree farm and the little tree is worried, asking the big tree, "Dad, what are we going to do? They're going to cut us down!" So I cut the little tree down and Phil cuts down the big tree. The two trees end up falling on us and killing us both.

Now even though I auditioned for two of the plays, I did a third play involving a completely polluted Hudson River.

It was great having the opportunity to turn in a third performance, but what I remember most is Frances Sternhagen's performance in one of the other plays. To this day it is one of the most phenomenal performances I've ever seen.

Trees with **Phil Bruns**

Sternhagen played an elementary school teacher in her classroom. The play was set during a time when most of the country was afraid the Russians were going to bomb the United States. School children had to perform drills where they would "take cover" under their desks, in the event the United States was attacked in an air raid. During the play there's an attack and Frances is trying to keep the kids calm while trying not to show her fear at the same time. She just owned the performance. The way she became that character…it was absolutely brilliant.

Foul was also the first job I'd done that got reviewed in the *New York Times*. I remember talking to my mom about it on the phone shortly after the *Times* came out. It was one of the few times I had impressed my parents.

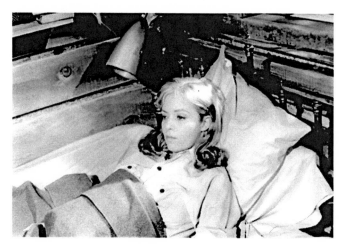

Scene from *Foul*

CHAPTER FIVE

Roommates Are the Best

I moved from my apartment on West Twenty-First Street and into a place across the street from the Ansonia Hotel on West Seventy-Third. It was a one-room apartment. I had a bathroom with a shower (no bathtub) and a very small kitchen. I didn't even have a bed, just a pull-out couch. However, at seventy-two dollars and fifty cents per month, I was able to afford the place with little issue.

After I moved I started working with a company called The Magic Mime Company of America. It was run by a man named Bob Capri. I quickly found it unsettling how most people involved with the company were in love with Bob. They would do anything and everything for this man. Some people would get his lunch, some people would simply sit at his feet; some were there just to be around for when he wanted to smoke pot. He once requested a very specific fabric for a robe he wanted to have made for himself. People in the company flocked the streets of New York, desperate to find this fabric so Bob could have his precious robe.

In a freakish way, he was like Charles Manson in how he set himself up as "master" of the mime company. Also, the appeal of Bob Capri was not unlike the appeal of Manson. They both brought together a group of rag-tag people all looking for something, some kind of life, a sense of belonging. Bob knew how to read people very well. He knew who he could go to for specific things. He knew exactly who he could manipulate and how. A big difference is Bob never asked anyone to steal or kill; however, a big similarity is they both eventually ended up incarcerated--Manson of course ended up in prison and Bob ended up in a mental institution.

In large part, this group of actors just adored Bob, similar to the way Manson got all those people to believe in him. I didn't quite fall into that group, but I was totally attracted to Bob's mind and his creativity.

We prepared a show for the Lincoln Center Library and his ideas were nothing short of fantastic. Little did I know that working with Bob would prepare me for working on *Helter Skelter*, when I played a member of Manson's Gang.

The best thing about working with the company was I met my soul sister, Joanne Sopko. After the Magic Mime Theatre closed down, all the actors went their separate ways. Jo and I opened our own company called The EiJo Mime Troupe. It was fun and we created some great sketches and did a bunch of shows, the best of which was a performance at a theatre on the East side. We also booked several parties but since it wasn't what we really wanted to do, we dissolved our little company and went back to looking for jobs.

Like Bonnie, Jo was just like me, just trying to make enough money to pay rent while trying to start a career. Soon we realized we could save even more money if we moved in together. So, Jo left her family home in Queens and moved into my apartment on West Seventy-Third Street. Now we had two pull-out sofas! Later we were given two beds. What a joy it was to sleep on a real mattress after months of feeling the springs of the fold-out couch twist into my back. I remember the first night, sliding between the sheets on a real bed. It's amazing how we quickly take for granted the simplest thing as a bed to sleep on.

My Front Door in NYC

Outside of My Apartment Building as it Looks Today

Soon we were living with two poodles and a cat. We each had our own dog; Jude the cat was shared. Once, Joanne's dog ate a whole lid of grass. The poor thing was never the same again. I swear it had hallucinations every day from then on. His ears would perk up and he'd twist his head this way and that, much the way a dog does when it hears a noise, except, the cat didn't react to these phantom noises. Neither did the other dog.

I'm not sure if Jo ever realized how much her friendship meant to me (and still does), but it was wonderful being able to spend time with a friend. Eventually we moved into an apartment on West Sixty-Fourth Street right across from Central Park, where we often brought the dogs. We would sit at an outdoor restaurant called The Monk's Inn and watch all the "fancy" people walk by on their way to Lincoln Center to see the ballet or the opera. We weren't jealous of those people, we simply enjoyed watching. We were very happy to be actresses, struggling or not. We were working. I shot a couple of commercials, made some decent money, enough to pay my share of the rent. We felt we had the world on a string. And I finally felt like I really belonged to something--a friendship.

We were lucky to be able to get the apartment on West Sixty-Fourth. A friend of ours lived in the apartment and wanted to move out. It was much bigger than our little garret we were living in and the rent was only $125 per month. It was a bit more than what we were already paying, but those were the days of rent control in New York. Rent Control is a rent stabilization program that basically says a landlord can only re-rent the space at a much bigger price when it becomes empty. So, we *unofficially* moved into our friend's place, an apartment that probably rents for about $3,500 per month today.

The apartment was part of a huge managerial firm and its representative was this fat, little, horny man who developed a crush on Jo. He wore a thin moustache that always grossed me out. He would come to the apartment every day around seven-thirty in the morning and ask for our friend, Matt. Unbeknownst to him, Matt was long gone and Joanne, who had been signing the rent checks under her name, was adding Matt's name under her name, so it looked like all three of us were living there (Note: If a landlord, accepts a check from the same person three months in a row, *that* person is now considered a statutory tenant). So he'd come over, ask for Matt and Joanne would immediately start crying, hysterically. That's when I would say, "Don't ask, please. Matthew didn't come home again last night. She's really upset. Please, don't ask about Matthew again." Anyway, I'm sure he caught on to our scheme eventually, but he probably just gave up. He thought we were sweet anyway.

One year, around Christmas, there was an oil strike. We had to live in our kitchen and use the gas stove as our only heat source for four days before the strike was finally settled. We even put our Christmas tree in the kitchen.

The first night it was actually kind of lovely. We would then run to the bedroom and snuggle under the covers making the dogs sleep with us to keep us warm. However, waking up in the cold, with stiff backs, and dogs slobbering all over our faces got old after the first night. Needless to say, we were happy to finally be able to turn the heat on.

Jo was a fantastic actress but she never had the hardcore "business" sense. She was definitely an artist though. Unfortunately, as all actors eventually come to realize, acting is an occupation. Just as professional athletes must understand sports is a business as much as it is a game, acting is a business just as much as it's an art. That's why I was out on the street all the time, trying to find work. Acting was a high for me (and still is) so I tried to get work as often as possible in order to sustain that high.

Working for a Living

People talk about the typical "starving actor," or the "starving artist" when referring to a down-on-his/her-luck actor or musician or other aspiring artist. Fortunately, we didn't have to starve because Jo and I got jobs working part-time as waitresses at a place called the Carnegie Delicatessen, which sat right under Carnegie Hall.

We worked daytime hours, which was nice because it still allowed us to do plays at night. And since we only worked the lunch shift, we were also able to go out on auditions.

I was never a good waitress but I learned quickly how to spot the men who wanted to be flirted with verses those who didn't want to flirt. As a waitress pretending to be an actress *pretending* to be a waitress, I always found the ones who flirted and had a good sense of who wanted to be left alone.

The Union waitresses didn't like us though. After all, they were full-timers. We were actors, in between jobs, so they saw us as encroaching on their customers, taking their wages and tips. Plus, we were younger with a lot more perk, and customers responded well to us.

The cook who worked the day shift just loved the two of us and he absolutely adored Jo. He was this loud, blustery, German man. He used to sweat a lot and his face was always red since it was hot in the kitchen, and he had to stand over the even-hotter stove all day. But he treated us very well. Whenever we had orders he was always quick to turn them around. Whenever we needed something extra he'd stop what he was doing, take care of us, and then get back to work. This always irked the veteran waitresses. He also flirted with us all the time. Naturally, we'd flirt back. Hey, if it helped us get our food even faster, it could only help with bigger tips. He even asked out Jo a few times but she always politely turned him down, saying she had a boyfriend or she was seeing someone. He would say, "Well you let me know when you're single and we'll go out some time." I'm pretty sure Jo stayed "in a relationship" the entire time we worked there.

At the end of our shifts we would sit at one of the now empty tables and count our tip money in front of the other waitresses. Looking back on it, that was pretty mean. But at the time we were young and we didn't care. We both knew the job would only last until we got our next acting gig.

Jo and I also worked at a place called The Sacred Cow, on Seventy-Second and Broadway. The dinners there were fabulous. Even before we worked there, we would occasionally go there and have dinner when we could afford it.

Our uniform was a white buttoned-down shirt, short black skirt, and fishnet stockings. I hated those stockings. They made me feel cheap. I had to take orders, serve food and wipe the crumbs off the tablecloth. I ended up getting fired for accidentally sweeping crumbs right onto the lap of a customer. He got pissed and complained to the woman who ran the place. She brought me into the back, told me I was no longer needed, and that was that. All in all, I had lasted a total of two nights.

Losing that job didn't break my heart though. I felt free again. And living in New York was great. Along with the benefits of rent control, I didn't own a car so I didn't have to worry about car insurance. And I was so young; I didn't worry about health insurance either. Jo and I decided to eat macrobiotic and lived on brown rice, vegetables and tuna fish. That diet lasted until we found out there was mercury in tuna fish.

I never really felt like I was good at waitressing so I tried some other jobs to help pay the bills. I filled out voter forms. This got old *real* fast--I began making them up before I decided it wasn't for me. Jo and I also sold belts and wallets at a small roadside stand on Broadway until the cops made us leave. I have no idea where the stuff came from. Jo knew but she would never tell me. Call it a case of ignorance being bliss. Anyway, our little belt/wallet stand lasted two days before we were shut down. An officer came by and told us we couldn't sell items on the street without a license. That was a relief. I thought we were going to be arrested. So we asked him what we needed to do to get a license. It turned out obtaining a license would have cost more than it was worth, so we closed up shop and that job was done.

I worked for a temp agency once. I sat in front of a typewriter all day and addressed envelopes. Sounds pretty simple, but back in those days, there were no computerized templates, no forms. Not to mention, it's a hell of a lot harder to type on a typewriter than it is to type on a computer. There was no, "point-and-click" back them. No "click-and-print." I had to type every envelope individually. One day, shortly after I started, I simply got up and walked out of the office. I didn't tell anyone, not even my boss. I figured if I couldn't make a living as an actress and I had to do *this* for the rest of my life, I might as well give up. So I left. It was the last time I ever worked in an office.

I feel very fortunate I never had to succumb to the daily grind of working nine-to-five. I never had to work in a building where you couldn't open the windows and the only view was that of a fresh coat of "asylum-white" paint on the walls. I never took for granted what I had with acting. That's why I never rested. I never stopped to reminisce about my last acting job. When one was over, I only focused on moving on to the next.

Steambath

With *David Holzman's Diary*, I'd managed to perform a nude scene without ever getting hassled about it by either my parents or my friends. After *Diary*, I didn't really plan on doing any more nude scenes during my career. But I guess that's kind of the way it goes--you never really see these things coming. Likewise, and much like with *Diary*, I didn't see this one coming, either. Well, kinda, but not really...

Steambath was another extraordinary production filled with legendary performers like Anthony Perkins and Hector Elizondo I didn't get the part right away when I auditioned for *Steambath* so I was surprised when I got the call. These were the days long before answering machines (and even longer before cellular telephones). So, had I not been home at the time, I would have never gotten the part.

I was sitting around my apartment one Sunday afternoon when the phone rang. It was the producer. He told me an actress had to leave the production and, if I wanted in, I had to meet them immediately down at the Truck and Warehouse Theatre. They only promised me about five or six lines--a very small role--but I would also understudy the lead actress. I said yes, grabbed my stuff and jumped on the subway to go downtown.

Even though *Steambath* was being produced as an off-Broadway play, the actors had been contracted at a Broadway salary. This was done because the producers were so sure *Steambath* would be a huge hit and they didn't want to have to renegotiate everybody's salaries. Also many actors have what they call a "pay or play" clause in their contract. This means the actor must be paid for the run of the show whether s/he is fired or not. This clause really came into play as, one by one, every lead actor was let go.

Tony Perkins signed on to direct the play. Dick Shawn was hired and fired long before the play ever made it to previews. So was Rip Torn. However, when Charles Grodin was hired as lead actor, he managed to stay long enough to make it into the previews. But that was only because Tony had to leave for California to shoot a film; the delay on *Steambath* was so long Tony had to be on the set of his next project. When he left, the producers felt the show had to continue so they hired a new director, Jacques Levy, and Chuck Grodin, despite all the previous lead actors being fired, thought the lead role was his permanently.

Blonde Headshot for *Foul* and *Steambath*

Charles had it locked until Tony came back. Unfortunately, they ended up firing poor Chuck and Tony came back and played the lead *and* directed the show. I remember Chuck asking me years later in Los Angeles, in that playful, pouty way only Chuck Grodin can, "Eileen, why did I get fired? What did I do wrong?" In fact, he hadn't done anything wrong. Tony simply wanted to play the lead and Chuck had filled in for him while Tony had been on the west coast.

I had a small part in the second act during which I had to push a wheelchair across the stage, carrying another actor. A low-stress role with little visibility, but since I was a late addition, I was just happy to be a part of it. Not to mention, I had a blast being surrounded by all these wonderful actors *and* I was making a wonderful salary every week ("as the crow flies," as it's said in the theatre, being you get paid every Friday night).

I also understudied the lead actress. The producer had mentioned previously it was an understudy role, but it wasn't until we had begun rehearsals when I found out about the nude scene.

The lead actress was a very tall, busty, beautiful woman, with a high squeaky voice. People cruelly said God gave her breasts instead of brains. By all accounts, she had the perfect body for this role. In a scene where she has to take a shower prior to entering the steam bath, she would enter the shower and let her towel drop very slowly off her shoulders, down her arms, past her waist and eventually onto the floor. It was all very seductive and she performed it well. I can only assume she truly enjoyed being naked because, let me tell you...she took some *long* showers.

I never thought about that scene much beyond her performance because, as an understudy, I never thought I'd have to perform it. Of course, that day did come for me.

One night she was unable to show up, for personal reasons, so I ended up taking my first lead in the show. My roommate, Jo, was in the audience that night, as she'd come to support me.

During the shower scene, while everybody was expecting this long, drawn out, sexy performance, I took the fastest shower you could possibly imagine. I lathered, rinsed, but dared not repeat. I might have even been out of the shower before my towel even hit the floor; it was that quick. Jo, who was sitting close to the front, told me afterward she'd heard a husband and wife talking about the scene. The husband had said, "I thought it would be embarrassing to see someone naked on stage but I didn't even know she was nude."

Tony Perkins, one of the nicest and most encouraging people I've ever met, was quite the jokester during *Steambath*. He loved to play pranks on the other actors during and between performances. During one particular performance, which just happened to be another time the lead actress was off, and during my shower scene, I remember looking briefly offstage. I noticed Tony Perkins standing there, waiting for his cue. Now, nothing of this seemed out of the ordinary, until I noticed him looking at me. It was kind of eerie. He was just standing there, staring at me very intently. Then, he raised his hand toward his neck and, with his finger, he made a slicing motion across his throat. Imagine, if you will, standing in a shower, fully naked, and looking offstage as Norman Bates is making the international hand signal for, "I'm going to cut your throat!" It took all of me not to crack up in the middle of the show.

Love Me or Leave Me…But Please Love Me

Joyce Carol Oates' *Ontological Proof of My Existence* was based on one of Oates' short stories, *How I Contemplated the World from the Detroit House of Correction and Began My Life Over Again*, and the novel *Wonderland*. This was the show that was to change my life forever.

It's about a young, misdirected girl named Shelly who leaves Detroit and moves to New York to find love. She meets a guy in the bus station and he takes her to his downstairs grotto-like apartment and turns her into his prisoner. The man eventually brings over other men to have sex with her. Shelly, desperate for love and to please this man, accepts the guys that come to the apartment as lovers. She also pretends to be a young boy, at the wishes of her pimp lover. Shelly has no problem succumbing to the pimps as long as he loves her. Being I was very androgynous, I fit the role perfectly.

I found out about this audition the same way I found out about many of my stage auditions--up at The Actor's Equity Office. I took one look at the audition notice and knew I could play this part. God knows I knew how it felt to be invisible, just as Shelly felt when she was at home in Detroit.

We were performing in a small, ninety-nine seat theatre called The Cubiculo on the West side of Manhattan. The name of the theatre was taken from a line in a Shakespeare Play where the character says, "Shall we go to The Cubiculo?" It's a play with only three characters; Shelly, Martin the pimp, and Shelly's father, who comes from Detroit to take her home. The father comes with a slide projector and shows Shelly pictures of herself as a child while she sits in a corner.

I didn't get paid for my part in the play, but that was fine. Again, it was all about performing. However, the frosting on the top of this cake came in the form of a review in *Newsweek* magazine.

I also received a letter from Ms. Oates telling me how excited she was that I was doing her play. She had written about how she had envisioned me and how stunned she was by how much I looked like her. Carol Kane, who had also auditioned for Shelly, opened the show with two other actors and read poetry.

Martin Gage and Fifi Oscard of The Fifi Oscard Agency had read the reviews in *Newsweek* and *Backstage*. They came down to see my performance one night and, after the show, they caught up with me and asked me to join their agency. I was flattered. Of course, I accepted their offer not knowing they would be among the most instrumental people in my entire life. I had no idea they would eventually line up the most important audition of my career.

Psychic Predictions

I visited a psychic once. It was after I had done *Steambath*. I met a woman named Mrs. Carvainis, at the Ansonia Hotel in Manhattan. I wasn't much into psychics or their practice, but a friend dared me to get "read," so, off I went.

When I arrived at the hotel, I remember standing just outside debating whether or not to simply turn around and go back home. What the hell was I doing there? Did I really believe a psychic was going to be able to tell me whether or not I'd be a famous actress? Did I really believe my fate rested in the premonitions of some lady gazing into a crystal ball? Probably not. Although I did think about all the ghosts of showbiz celebrities who allegedly still resided in the Ansonia Hotel and I wondered if I would run into any.

After very little self-debate, I walked inside. I figured I had nothing to fear by doing this. Sure, I probably cursed a bit more than I should, but who doesn't swear every once in a while? I'd never broken any of the Ten Commandments. OK, maybe one or two, but never any of the *big* ones. The only thing I would need to consider would be how much of this woman's prophecies I would actually believe. That would be on me, not her.

I took the elevator to a fourth floor apartment and knocked on the door. The door opened slowly and standing there was Mrs. Carvainis. Now, it's been some years since I saw this psychic, but I want you to try something: Close your eyes. Now imagine an old lady who's a psychic, perhaps from a movie you might have seen. You got her? Good. Because THAT'S her! Seriously! She wore a black dress; she had white spindly, wispy hair, twisted up into a bun. Her skin was wrinkled and sagging in places. And I swear, her pupils must have been dilated only minutes before I knocked because she had these strangely huge black eyes.

But, stereotypes aside, I walked into the apartment. She led me through what I assumed to be her living room and into a study where we sat down at a table. She called me Eileen Scott - a stage name I used during filming of *Teenage Gang Debs* - which is the name I had given her over the phone. At first I thought, *a real psychic would have called me by my true name*, but I shrugged it off.

After tracing her index finger over my palm for a bit, she made her first prediction: "I see good fortune for you." *Well that's a good start*, I thought. Who doesn't want "good" and "fortune" in their future? But I kept my excitement in check. She continued to tell me she saw cameras and lights. Then she guessed I was an actress. However, in her thick, Romanian accent, it sounded more like, "ecktriss." It may have even been phony, but if it was, it was good enough to fool me.

She then proceeded to tell me if I stayed on my current path, I would reach the top of my profession. More good news. She even went so far as to mention contracts and lots of money. Even MORE good news. At this point, I began to think she was probably just telling me what I wanted to hear, but it was hard not to feel a little excitement over her predictions. But then, she told me something I hadn't expected.

She talked about negative forces; forces that were trying to bring me down. "Demonic forces," to be exact. That was about the time I looked at my watch and thought it was time to go. What the hell was this woman talking about? *Demonic forces, really?* I wanted to believe it was absurd, but when someone you don't know tells you demonic forces are trying to harm you in some way, you tend to listen. Or at least, I did. Mrs. Carvainis advised me to trust in my beliefs and, in order to stay on the right path, I needed to see both the good and bad sides of what I was doing.

After the demonic talk she dug into my past. She talked about how I wasn't appreciated as a child and about how I strove to be noticed more. *Not bad*, I thought, but not much of a stretch either considering actors are some of the most insecure and narcissistic people on the planet. But still, I continued to give Mrs. Carvainis the benefit of the doubt. Then, she produced a pack of Tarot cards.

Now, the deal with Tarot Cards, as explained to me by a friend, is that Tarot is subject to various methods of interpretation. So basically, you shouldn't read into it too much. However, the process is pretty much the same each time: Every reading involves three things; a questioner, an interpreter, and the cards. Sometimes the questioner asks questions directly, sometimes s/he does not. During my reading with Mrs. Carvainis, I was not given the opportunity to ask any questions. She simply shuffled the cards and dealt. Naturally, I felt a fair amount of shock, and even a little fear, when she drew the Death card.

Mrs. Carvainis spoke about financial matters, personal achievements--she didn't even touch on the Death card until I asked her. She downplayed it a bit, told me this card didn't always imply death, it could also mean change or misfortune. "Change or misfortune" didn't sound all bad. I could handle that. As an actress, I'd experienced quite a bit of change, even up to that point in my career. And a misfortune could be--wait a second...wouldn't *death* be considered a misfortune? What was this lady playing at? I decided to ask her if she believed in fairies or elves. The kinds of things found in fantasy stories. She told me she believed in doppelgangers, and that was about the time my skin began to crawl.

The Ansonia Hotel as it Looks Today

The thought of another Me walking around this earth was somewhat terrifying. The Jewish equivalent of a doppelganger; *dybbukim*, is a soul that enters another person's body and doesn't leave until exorcised by religious rite. Sounds like a wonderful thing to believe in, doesn't it? Well, I was finished with the topic. I switched gears and asked her if she saw me winning an Academy Award in the future. She got up from the table, looked at her watch, and kindly motioned toward the door. It was time for me to leave.

CHAPTER SIX

The Call of Pazuzu

I wish I could say it was a dark and stormy night when Fifi Oscard called me about the part in *The Exorcist*. Or, that I felt something in the air, like some strange, supernatural presence beckoning me to audition for the role. But it was a day like any other day. I was at home by myself when she called. I wasn't expecting her call so when I heard her voice, I was immediately excited. Whenever Fifi called, it was usually to talk about an audition or a job, and this time proved to be no different.

She told me there was a movie being shot in New York--a major Hollywood motion picture. The movie was to be based on a book about a twelve-year old girl who gets possessed by a demon. She said the casting director, Juliet Taylor, was looking for someone small and strong. I thought it was kind of strange at first because, although I was certainly small for my age, I didn't know if I'd be able to pull off the part of a twelve-year old. But Fifi said not to worry, they already had a young girl for the part; they now needed someone who could play the role

103

of the demon that possesses this little girl. She said Taylor wanted a girl, a bit older, but similar in size and height to the little girl already cast to play the twelve-year old. She asked me if I thought I could do it. I had never turned down anything up to this point in my career so I said yes. She told me to meet Juliet at her office the next day. Sounded simple enough to me.

When I finally hung up the phone, I suddenly heard Mrs. Carvainins' voice in my head. *"Demonic forces…"* Maybe the old woman had some psychic ability after all.

The following morning I hopped on a bus and went downtown to Juliet Taylor's office. I wondered what she was going to ask me. I only had a brief description of the role, provided by Fifi, but I assumed we would talk about it more when I got there. I'd hoped I had what she was looking for.

I got to Juliet's building a little early and her secretary walked me right into her office. Juliet had me sit across from her desk. She was very professional and polite. She asked me what kinds of films I enjoyed watching and which ones I enjoyed making. I told her I enjoyed all kinds of films. I told her my passion was for acting and it didn't matter what kind of movie it was. As long as I had the opportunity to act, I was going to give it 110 percent.

We talked a lot about horror films. We discussed the way good, classic horror movies are able to bring that raw fear and intensity to the screen. It was then she mentioned a book called, *The Exorcist*, by William Peter Blatty. She'd asked me if I'd heard of it. I told her I had heard about the book and that my agent had mentioned it to me as well. Juliet said if I was interested in auditioning for the movie, I'd have to read the book first to get an idea of what was going to be needed for the part. She asked me if I had a copy of the book. I lied and said, "Yes." I wanted her to believe I was prepared and ready to research the role as thoroughly as possible. She then asked me if I'd be able to finish it that night and come back the next day. I told her I absolutely would finish it for the next day. Inside, I thought, *I hope so.*

When I left Juliet's office I immediately raced to the nearest bookstore, located a copy of *The Exorcist*, bought it, and ran back to my apartment on Sixty-Fourth Street, across from Lincoln Center. I was a walker in those days and generally made my way around the city on foot, often running through Central Park; partly to stay in shape, partly because I was always in a hurry. So, with my package tucked under my arm, I declined all means of transportation--bus, train, taxi. I ran up Fifth Ave to Fifty-Ninth Street, turned up the side of Central Park, right on Central Park West, entered my humble abode, hurried up the stairs to my third floor apartment, ran straight into my bedroom, stripped off my clothes in favor of some sweats, closed the door, lay down on my bed, and proceeded to read Blatty's *The Exorcist* from cover to cover.

I didn't come out of my room until I was finished.

My first impression of the book was one of awe; awe and sheer terror. I mean, that book scared the bejesus out of me! I loved every word and every page of it, but it was surely terrifying. Since I was brought up atheist, I was raised to believe there is no God and no Devil. I'd always felt there is *something*, but I wasn't religious in any way, so I can't really explain my beliefs other than to say I believed there was some *thing* or some supreme being, but we, as humans, just cannot understand it.

I've always enjoyed reading. One of my earliest memories is of reading Daphine Du Maurier's *The Birds* when I was still a kid. As good as Hitchcock's movie was, the book made the hair on the back of my neck stand up when I read it. As I read *The Birds*, I would imagine the sound of birds' claws scratching at the roof of my parents' house, the constant flutter of wings, flapping all around my room and around my head. It was unnerving. To this day I am afraid of more than two birds in a single space.

Upon reading *The Exorcist* for the first time, I immediately felt that same feeling, as if something very evil was afoot. The torture that poor girl went through; it tore at me as if it were real. I found I was constantly telling myself, *This is only a book...it's only a book. This didn't really happen.* Of course, as most people already know, the book is based on a true story; the story of a little boy who was possessed by a demon. Blatty turned the boy into a girl, Regan, because he believed a little blond girl would be more frightening and he didn't want to have anything to do with the original boy in his story.

The characters leaped right off the pages, incredibly alive and real. I knew exactly who his characters were. I understood the mother and I could feel how passionate and desperate she was about finding help for her daughter. I understood the young priest's confusion about his own faith and his guilt over his mother and his reluctance to accept what was really happening to young Regan. And I could understand the needs and commitment of the old priest, to find this demon he'd been searching for most of his life and to exorcise it.

Most of all, I understood the pain of a child not having her whole family around to help her. I also recognized the idea that a little girl, so deprived of parental attention, was perhaps imagining the evil in order to gain the attention she so longingly craved. Blatty painted a beautifully horrific picture of a demonic presence that was equal parts psychological and supernatural. You see, the book is really ambivalent on this matter and leaves it up to the reader to decide whether Regan is truly possessed by a demon or has severe mental issues. In fact, during the death scene, as written in the book, the demon's eyes do not go from Regan's into Father Karras' just before Karras jumps out the window. During the final struggle in the movie, however, the demon that once inhabited Regan moves on to possess

Father Karras and his eyes become green and his face changes to an evil, deathly pallor.

Upon finishing the final page of the book, I immediately knew I could play the demon that possesses this child, and I set out to prepare for my audition.

I actually felt a kind of "connection" to the little girl, which is certainly strange, considering she was twelve and I was no longer a teenager. And while she did not have any siblings, I felt her situation was similar to mine while growing up in Bayside: just a sweet, innocent girl, caught in tragic circumstances--totally arbitrary to that of my twin sister--that were neither a result of my own doing, nor within my repair. And although I was never religious, I always thought if there was a God, he was surely an evil god, and one that meted out punishment to little girls who were bad. I never thought of him as a kindly soul. This was not a part of Regan's beliefs, of course. It was simply an idea I had struggled with as a child and then, later on, as an adult. It certainly helped me play the part of one of God's fallen angels.

Becoming a Demon

So I started to wonder about how I was going to portray a little girl possessed by a demon. I tried to imagine how a demon might act--how the *devil* might act. I began to picture wild beasts, gnashing and clawing, the ripping of flesh. I

108

decided to visit the public library and check out some books that showed pictures of wild animals in their most intense, ferocious states. The act of predators attacking and mutilating smaller animals seemed demonic to me.

I brought the books back to my apartment and shut myself in my bedroom once again. I pulled the shades down on all the windows, lit some candles on the floor, and got up onto my bed. I set one of the books down on the bed sheet, opened to a page of animals attacking each other. From there, I imagined myself a wild animal.

For the moment I tried to forget everything I knew about human movement and choreography. I closed my eyes, threw my hands up over my head and clawed at the air. I arched and twisted my back in ways that were so painful, but I kept going. I imagined myself as a wild beast, chasing after some defenseless prey. And then, I imagined myself as the same wild beast, trapped inside the skin of another. I was trying to escape from a prison of flesh and bone and innocence. At one point, I opened my eyes and looked at my shadow along the wall. The candles, flickering all around the foot of the bed, had animated my own being into something I'd never seen before. And I thought if my own movements were even half as gross, evil and disturbing as what I saw against my walls, I just might be able to pull this off.

The following day, I went back to Juliet's office for my official audition. I'd read Blatty's book, cover to cover. I felt good about my interpretation of a demon, trapped within a human soul that I'd rehearsed the night before. I felt ready. Of course, no audition, no matter how confident you may feel, is ever as it seems.

"I would like for you to improvise the little girl AND the demon inside of her," Juliet said after I sat down in her office. "Both?" I asked. I tried to make it sound more like a simple confirmation and less like surprise. "Both," Juliet said. I hadn't exactly prepared for both auditions, but I'd done plenty of improvisation before, on stage and during my brief career as a mime. So, I took a few deep breaths, collected myself, and began my audition.

I got up from the chair, and moved it to the side. Then I walked back toward the middle of her office, and dropped to my knees. I started to whimper and cry. In that moment, I was a helpless twelve-year old girl pleading for her mother's assistance. "Mommy! Mommy! Help me, please!" I begged in the very best, high-pitched, twelve-year old voice I could muster. Then, I contorted into a very uncomfortable, twisted position and the next thing I knew, this horrible, low, guttural voice came from my belly: "*You're mine, you sow!!! You're mine, you pig! Get away from her!*"

In my mind, I had now transformed Juliet's office into Regan's room. I was in her bedroom, trying to rid myself of the demon that had forced itself inside of me. Then I *was* the demon, demanding control, swearing at everyone who was in the room. And then Regan again. Sweet, innocent, little Regan, tortured by some evil, twisted being. And then became the demon, one last time; writhing and reaching for control, attempting to force out all the good and innocence left inside Regan's body.

When it was over I opened my eyes. I was back in Juliet's office, kneeling on the floor in front of her desk. Across from me Juliet sat in her chair, her mouth dropped open. I tried not to react at all to this. I didn't want to show any kind of over-confidence in my performance. I simply stood from the floor, pulled the chair from the wall and sat back down. I acted as cool as I could. Deep down though, I felt I'd done a great improv. Actually, I knew it.

Juliet said it was a good interpretation and she wanted me to meet the director, William Friedkin. I told her that would be wonderful. She set a date and told me I would be meeting William as well as the girl who would be playing Regan, Linda Blair, Linda's mother, and the makeup artist, Dick Smith. She said she'd call me to let me know where the meeting would be.

And then she asked me something I hadn't expected. She asked me to, "tighten up" a little. I knew she meant, "Lose weight," and that was the strange part. I still very much had a genderless body and I was by no means fat. However, Juliet went on to explain further; in order to look like a twelve-year old girl, I'd have to shrink down, just a bit, so there would be no discrepancy at all between our size differences. I told her it wouldn't be a problem. If a casting director asks you to lose weight, you lose weight. Period.

So, skinny little Eileen had to figure out a way to "tighten up" in a very short period of time. I only had a day or two before I would meet the director and the others. I thought about running more, taking even more stairs and fewer elevators than before. And then an idea hit me.

In the early 1970s there were these plastic suits that were made for people who were very serious about losing weight quickly. They were advertised in the back of romance magazines and the tabloids, aka "movie magazines." Well, with my limited financial income and time budgets, I knew I didn't have enough money to buy one of those suits, so I grabbed a box of saran wrap from a drawer at home, wrapped my body over and over in plastic and then took to my bicycle and rode up and down Central Park. I rode for hours. Occasionally I stopped, but only to either re-wrap the plastic even tighter or to pull open the pieces that wrapped around my ankles just enough to allow the sweat to drain from my homemade suit.

And man, did I sweat! Perspiration poured from my plastic suit like a slow faucet. I drank nothing but water, day and night. I cut down to one small meal a day, like a yogurt or a piece of fruit. I didn't own a scale, so in a way I was blind, and all I could do was hope my weight-loss efforts would be enough.

Other Things I Did to Stay "Tightened Up"

My other agent, Martin Gage, Fifi's partner, called me shortly after the meeting with Juliet and told me how much Juliet liked me. I was ecstatic. But, Martin reminded me this was only the first of multiple steps so I took it in stride and remained focused. He asked me about the weight-loss thing. He said Juliet had "recommended" I lose a few pounds. I told

Martin I'd been fasting and working out like a maniac every day. He said that was fine and what mattered most was that I be able to tighten up for the actual filming. Sure, it would be great to tighten up before I met Bill Friedkin, but it was likely I wouldn't have enough time. So, as long as I was fit for the shoot I was all set.

I felt a little stress roll off my shoulders when he said that. I'd still continue to ride around New York City wearing my Saran Wrap Suit, but at least I knew it wouldn't make or break me being cast in the film.

Meeting Billy, Linda and Dick

I walked into the hotel located on Fifth Avenue, directly opposite from my apartment and separated only by a massive park. The lobby was made of marble; marble walls, a marble registration desk in the back. The place reeked of money. There were potted flowers everywhere. Beautiful men and women, dressed to kill, traversed the space--their heels clicking along the marble floor.

I weaved my way through the crowd in my sneakers and little dress and looked for the elevator. Somewhere in a room up on the top floor, was Director, Bill Friedkin. The youngest director to win an academy award. I'd be lying if I said I wasn't a little intimidated. I had seen *The French Connection*. The man clearly had a talent for making a great movie. He also had a talent for putting the right people in the right places. And as I took the elevator to the top floor, I silently hoped I would be one of those people in *The Exorcist*.

The elevator doors opened. The room I sought was all the way down at the end of the hall. It was then I had one of those, "now or never" moments. When you either freak out, turn around then run away as fast as you can, or you slow yourself, relax, and take a deep breath. I took a deep breath and got off the elevator. *I'm going to be fine*, I told myself as I walked down the hall toward Friedkin's room. I tried to remain cool and poised but, as an actress, there's always that five percent of your brain, buried just below the section containing your confidence, which says, *What if they don't like me?*

I knocked on the door to the room. A man opened it. To this day, I do not recall his name, but standing--or rather, *pacing*--just behind him, was Bill Friedkin. He paced a lot. And he chewed on his fingernails. I'm not entirely sure why, either. I think he's just one of those people who can't relax. Who's uncomfortable about a given project up until the day the project is finished. Even on the set, he was always pacing. For a moment, I almost felt like I knew what he was feeling.

A woman sitting on a couch stood up and extended her hand to me. "Hi, I'm Elinore Blair, Linda's mother."

I shook her hand and said, "Hello."

"This is Linda," she said.

I shook Linda Blair's hand for the first time. And while I knew they had been looking for someone of the same height and size as Linda, I was still surprised how when she stood from the couch, we met eye-to-eye. It wasn't exactly like I was staring into a mirror, but there were a lot of similarities. Her hair, though a different color than mine, fell onto her shoulders just like mine did. Her arms were about the same size and length as mine. Our waists were also fairly tiny and equal in size, but her legs were a bit skinnier. After all, I was no longer a teenager. About the only difference was our faces, but I figured some crazy makeup artist would probably take care of that.

At this point, Friedkin stopped pacing long enough to come shake my hand as well. "Juliet has told me a lot about you," he said. I just smiled and tried to act cool.

We all sat down and talked for a while about the movie. Friedkin spoke about how the film was based on a book by William Peter Blatty. I felt it would be rude if I tried to cut in and let him know I read the book, so I let him talk. He said Linda would be the primary actress, playing the part of Regan MacNeil, the girl possessed by a demon, but the film needed someone similar in size to Linda. He said this was because of a scene Linda simply couldn't perform due to her age--a scene that was considered inappropriate for a twelve-year old. Having read the book, I was pretty sure I already knew what scene he was referring to.

After we chatted, he told me Dick Smith wanted to ask me some questions. Dick wore glasses, and I remember regarding him simply as a plain-looking man. He stood up and extended his hand. "Hi, I'm Dick Smith. It's very nice to meet you," he said, shaking my hand. He had the kindest eyes I'd ever seen in a man, along with a very gentle smile. And when he shook my hand, he did so with both his hands, firmly, but at the same time, delicately. He was a very nice man and, upon meeting him for the first time, I was even more eager to work on this film knowing I'd likely be working with him quite often.

"I'd like you to come up to my studio," Dick said. He told me about his studio just outside of New York City which was where he did most of his effects work. Dick had worked with many actors there in the past for different movies and TV shows. He told me about how he'd made what's called a "life mask" of Linda's face and that he needed to make one for me as well.

Dick Smith used a layering technique including different latex prosthetics for the scars on Regan's face. And in order to make everything look believable, he needed to make a mask for me--to make sure the scars were in exactly the same places.

"Absolutely," I told him. And with that, the meeting was over. My journey into Bill Blatty's world had finally begun.

Next stop: The Magical Makeup and Effects Studio of Dick Smith.

With Rick Baker and Dick Smith (Years Later)

CHAPTER SEVEN

The Brilliant, and Mad, Science of Dick Smith

I took the train to a town just outside New York City to meet Dick Smith in his studio. My agents, Fifi Oscard and Martin Gage, had asked me to keep them in the loop with what was going on. I told them I had to go to Dick Smith's laboratory where he was going to make something called a "life mask."

When the train stopped, I got off and grabbed a cab. I was so excited to get started, I asked the cab driver to "step on it, please." The driver stared back at me through the rear-view mirror and said, "Lady, this place is only a coupla blocks from here. I think you're gonna be on time."

The cabbie let me off in front of the studio. When I knocked on the door, Dick himself let me in. He took me down some steps to his studio and what I saw next is something I never expected.

First off, there were life masks all over the place. It was as if the eye-less faces of Marlon Brando, Dustin Hoffman and Jack Palance stared at me; greeting me as I entered. There were

119

all kinds of foam latex pieces lying around and hanging from walls, neatly organized, mind you. It didn't seem as if anything was out of place. It was like walking through a museum; a gallery of all the famous people with whom he'd worked with over the years. I was totally star-struck and utterly speechless. I had to pinch myself to make sure it was all real.

Then Dick came from behind me. He shook my hand again and thanked me for coming. *Why is he thanking me for coming?* I thought. *I should be thanking him!* However, as time would pass, I would eventually come to understand this was just Dick's personality--an incredibly polite, genuine person.

We sat down for a bit and he went over the entire process with me. He said it would take about three hours to do it correctly. I hadn't planned anything else for the rest of the day so timing wasn't an issue. When he was done explaining, I got in, "the chair," and he went to work.

The first thing he did was lather up my face with Vaseline. This was so the compound used to make the mask wouldn't stick to my skin and would easily slide off once it was dry. I had to shut my eyes, of course, so for the next three hours I was essentially in the dark. He stuck a couple of straws up my nose so I would be able to breathe.

Many people find the process to be uncomfortable but I actually found it to be very peaceful, even restful. Dick told me Marlon Brando completely freaked out. He said Brando kept shooting the straws out of his nose and opening his eyes because he didn't like not being able to see what was going on. Brando was totally paranoid about the whole process and Dick had to pull the plaster off his face and sculpt the rest of it from photos. When you see Brando's makeup in *The Godfather* you would never think Dick had any challenges with his life mask.

Dick loved to talk about his career, school, and other movie and TV stars with whom he'd worked with in the past. But he never talked about his past with any sort of braggadocio. I think he just felt, since we were going to be there a while, it was a great way of passing the time, kind of like the way a hair dresser talks to her client while she's cutting hair. Except, Dick's "clients" weren't just everyday people, they were famous actors. And with every famous name he rattled off, I kept thinking to myself, *Is this really me? Am I really getting 'life-masked' by this Emmy Award-winning makeup artist? Will I be someone he talks about with the next person who sits in this chair?* I tried to take it all in as he continued to layer my face with more and more goop. I was in Heaven for the moment, and it didn't matter to me how long it would take.

After the mask was set and Dick peeled it off, he said he had what he needed for now, and the next thing he would is make sure my mask looked as close as possible to Linda's mask.

After he sent me on my way, and as I was walking back to the train, it still didn't feel quite "real." It was like make-

121

believe, a fantasy world, and I was simply a guest in this wonderful universe. But it was a great feeling and one that I didn't want to end.

A few days later, I found out all the foam latex pieces (scars, cuts) on Linda's life mask fit my mask perfectly. Everything about our masks were identical; everything except for our noses. Linda's nose turned up like a pug nose and, during filming, all they had to do was tape up my nose to make sure they were as close to the same size as possible.

Makeup Tests Before the Shoot

Negotiations

Fifi Oscard and Martin Gage had already begun negotiations on the terms of my contract. This is typical. There's usually a round of negotiations up front, just after the audition, and then again after the screen test. This is so nobody has the upper hand when both sides negotiate the final agreement. The initial agreement for my contract was six weeks at $750 per week. The studio also wanted me for more than just one scene.

Now, I know what you're thinking: $750 per week isn't terrible, but it's far from great. However, considering this was 1972, $750 per week back then would be equal to about $3,590.00 in 2012! That doesn't seem like a bad payday now, does it?

Screen Test

We did the screen tests in an old two-story studio apartment in mid-town Manhattan. As soon as I arrived, the camera operator, First Assistant Director and the special effects people wanted to get moving on some of the effects that still needed to be tested.

The Assistant Director, Terry Donahue, told me, along with my screen test, we would be testing some spitting scenes. There's a scene in the movie when Regan spits some greenish-goo on Father Merrin's face. The special effects people had already decided to use green pea soup for the vomit but they didn't want the spit and vomit mixtures to be the same. For one, the green pea soup was very runny and, if used in the spitting scenes, would have simply run right down Max Von Sydow's face. They wanted something thicker that would stick a little longer, so we tested different stuff.

They had me sit down on a bed and I got ready to test the first mixture. Suddenly, I see the crew entering the room in raincoats and protective gear. They had even covered the cameras with plastic. Apparently a lot was expected of me and my spitting abilities. I thought I was only spitting on someone's face. Perhaps that was the idea, and the crew just expected I'd be spraying the stuff everywhere.

We tried a cottage cheese mixture first. Terry spooned a bit into my mouth and I was to hock the stuff at a man wearing a mask and a black trench coat. Funny thing is, I actually like cottage cheese so testing this wasn't so bad. The problem was the curds sort of separated when I spit it out and the stuff basically went everywhere. And I mean *everywhere*; on the furniture, on the floor, on Terry. Granted, that was going to happen, but this "spit-spreading" effect wasn't making the cut. It made it look like I was simply trying to spit something out rather than spit *at* someone. So they decided to try another mixture. The idea was to have a focused, somewhat congealed spit effect. What they came up with still makes me nauseous to this day.

I drink a cup of black coffee every day. I love coffee. However, I do NOT like milk or cream or any kind of dairy in my coffee. And though they didn't tell me what was in the mixture, my gag reflex was immediate: pancake batter and coffee. What's strange is, I enjoy pancakes. Even pancakes *with* coffee because you can't taste the milk since it's already cooked. However, thick, lumpy, oozing pancake batter, mixed with cold black coffee was almost enough to make me vomit for real.

For the pancake batter/coffee mixture, I couldn't wait to hock this shit out. As soon as Terry said to, I shot that stuff straight at the man wearing the trench coat. For the most part, the stuff was easier to spit in a controlled, focused manner, but it still went everywhere. So Terry asked me to try spitting in different ways. I didn't quite understand exactly how to spit "differently," but I tried a few more times. I was still pretty bad but I guess it worked because we moved on.

The next scene we tested was the crucifix masturbation scene. This was a little unnerving. The scene from the book was still fresh in my mind so I'd assumed the props folks would be bringing in a typical, normal-sized crucifix. The prop guy had a definite sense of humor. The crucifix they brought out was a good two feet long by one foot wide and made out of papier mache. I thought it was a prank at first. I thought, *Okay, ha-ha, these guys want to see a girl fake-rape herself with this thing, that's fine.*

Luckily for me, I also have a sense of humor and if the crew wanted to have a laugh at my expense, I had no problem with it.

But then Terry said, "Are you ready?" I looked at him, my smile having already disappeared and said, "Where's the real crucifix?" He told me, "It's in your hand. Let's do this." I stared at the monstrosity in my hands and my initial thought was, *Holy shit! What am I going to do with this?* But the crew stood there, waiting for me to perform, and I realized Terry was serious. They wanted me to do the test with the giant crucifix. On "Action," I immediately became Regan, possessed by the demon calling out for her mother. Then I was the demon, stabbing myself in the crotch with this huge crucifix. I reverted back to Regan again and so on. It was actually pretty fun, and much different from the scene used in the movie, but unfortunately, what we did during the test never made it into the film. Neither Linda nor I ever got to play the Demon writhing back and forth on the bed, going from a little girl to this demon that possessed her.

A Commercial, a Quaalude, and a Great Decision

After the screen test, I went back home to my apartment. It wasn't long after I'd gotten back home that Fifi called. She said they were very interested in me but they still needed to work out the terms on both sides. This was great news but I still wasn't sure exactly what they wanted me to do, or when they wanted me to do it.

So, the waiting game was back on for the moment. I tried not to dwell on *The Exorcist* and find work to stay busy and pay the bills. I shot a commercial for the Bryman Schools. The shoot was in Washington D.C. I remember flying down there, the whole time thinking, *I wonder if the people from The Exorcist will call.* I was so nervous they were going to call and I wouldn't be around. What if they called and I wasn't able to get back to them? Would they give up on me? Would they go and find someone else? Dick Smith had already made a life mask and I'd already done the screen tests, so they couldn't just find someone else. Could they?

This apprehension ended up interfering with my shoot for The Bryman Schools. It was a spokesperson ad. All I had to do was stand in front of a camera and say a few lines. It was something like, "I love my job. I go to the Bryman School. I am a Dental Hygienist and I love it." As simple as the lines were, I was really nervous. The client and the production company hated what I was doing on camera. Of course, we shot take after take after take. At one point a production assistant pulled me aside and said, "Take this; it will help calm you down." She was holding a small pill in her hand. I didn't know what it was and I didn't ask, I took it and swallowed it down. I figured it was some kind of over-the-counter muscle relaxer or something. Then the assistant told me it was a Quaalude. Well that wasn't what I had expected to hear. I thought she was joking around at first. Nope. I'd just swallowed perhaps the most favored drug of the 1970s. I'd heard of Quaaludes before but had never tried them. I knew people used them during sex because it was sort of an aphrodisiac. The last thing I wanted to feel at this point was sexy but the production assistant had just wanted me to relax so I could shoot the commercial. Very well, then.

For the rest of the shoot, you could say I felt NO anxiety. The producers even had me rehearse the scene a bit before we rolled tape again. This really helped me relax even more. By the time I got in front of the camera again, I didn't worry about anything and I realized I could see myself in the Camera lens, so I just acted to myself. I guess they liked it because the commercial ran for over two years. I never saw it because it only aired on the west coast.

Another opportunity came up for a kids' show with puppets. The show was in Boston. They had live hosts that would talk and interact with the puppets. I was still waiting to hear about *The Exorcist* so I asked Jo if she wanted me to recommend her for it. I thought she'd be better for the job anyway. She had always loved children. She ended up spending about six months doing the show. It was one of the highlights of Jo's life and she was so good in it. Not surprisingly, when she was a little older, she became a child psychologist. It also turned out to be one of the best career decisions of my life because I finally got the call from The Fifi Oscard Agency.

Jo, the Professional Psychologist

CHAPTER EIGHT

"Whooshee" Arrives in Washington D.C.

On a cold, dreary day in late November 1972, Fifi called me. "They want you on the set," she said. I swear I had an out-of-body experience at that moment, because I could see myself holding the phone to my ear, reacting to what Fifi Oscard had just told me. I froze for a second, both in anticipation of what the terms were going to be and for how long they wanted me on the set. When I finally asked Fifi, she said, "Two weeks. They only want you for the masturbation stuff since Linda is too young to do that." *Bummer*, I thought. The original agreement had been for six weeks. My time on the set would be short but at least I got the part! I remained excited about the prospect of working on the film. However, Fifi then added, "I told them, 'two weeks is fine, but you'll have to pay her for six.'" This sounded nice. After all, who doesn't love getting paid for longer than they're active on a project?

Fifi went on, "The studio of course said, 'no,' so ultimately everybody agreed to the original six weeks." (There was just one catch) "They want you in Washington D.C. tomorrow," she told me. I nearly freaked out.

"Why?" I asked.

"I don't know," she said, "but they said it's something important. They need you to fly out first thing tomorrow."

In a partial daze, I received the instructions and the tickets for the early morning flight so I would be in D.C in time to shoot the following night.

I was picked up at the airport by a car sent by the studio, and deposited at the hotel. That evening they sent a limo--I had never been in a limo before--to my hotel to pick me up and bring me to the set. I remember the driver walking around to the side of the car to open the door for me. Lee J. Cobb was sitting in there. I freaked. Here I am, some indie actress from New York City, about to jump into a limo with a world-famous actor. I didn't know what to say. But, Cobb was very kind. He asked me where I was from, what other stuff I'd done. I don't remember exactly what I said. I was probably more star-struck than anything, but we certainly had a conversation. I'm sure he didn't recognize any of the projects I'd worked on, but he didn't say it. He was very charming. He could tell I was nervous, though. I told him this was my first time working on major motion picture. It was a whirlwind, a blur.

He said, "Just try to relax, be yourself. Then, when you're in front of the camera, be someone else."

It made me laugh and helped loosen me up. Still, it was quite overwhelming to receive acting tips from Lee J. Cobb.

Lee was the one who attached the nickname, "Whooshee," to me. As the limo pulled up to the set that evening, there were tons of crew outside setting up. There were also a lot of bystanders just looking on, waiting to see which famous actor or actress would pull up next. Lee J. Cobb stepped out to quite a bit of fanfare. I could only imagine what it felt like to have people react in such a way to your arrival. When I exited the limo after him, I immediately began hearing hushed voices saying things like, "Who's that? Who's she?" From then on, Lee referred to me as "Whooshee." "*Whooshee, come on over here!*" he would say. He got a chuckle out of it every time. And it actually felt pretty special, having been personally nicknamed by *the* Lee J. Cobb.

We shot the nighttime scene when Father Merrin first arrives at the MacNeil residence. It was in Georgetown and it was shot at an actual house. It's the scene where Father Merrin (Max von Sydow) approaches the house, looks up, and sees a figure walk past a lit window. Two hours of shooting later, I was back in the limo and back at my hotel. I caught a flight back to NYC the next morning.

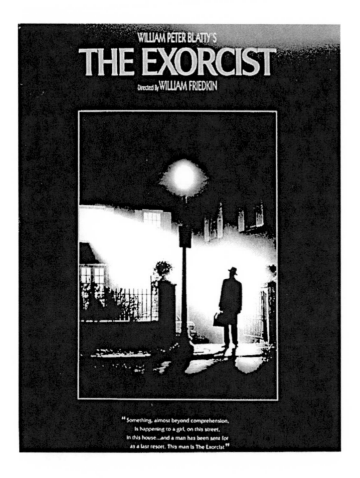

An image from the final shot actually ended up on the poster. Most people aren't aware it was me in the window, but I knew it. I was in a major motion picture. My dream was coming true. I shook off any memories of the psychic lady saying there would be trouble.

It was quite a trip when I saw that scene for the first time. To this day, it brings back the memory of sharing a limo with Lee J. Cobb. Unfortunately, we hadn't shot the scene together, but the conversation in the limo is one I've never forgotten.

When I got back to New York, I was told I would have to get fitted for fangs. The studio sent me to a dentist in order to take a mold of my teeth. Apparently, the dentist I saw had done this kind of thing before. So he knew I was an actress before I even got in the chair. Obviously, he didn't recognize me, which was evident when he asked me, "Have you been in anything I would recognize?" It was likely he didn't get out to too many plays or see many independent films. And that was all right. I was well aware mine wasn't a household name.

I told him, "I've done some theater and mostly smaller productions." He nodded as he told me to open wide and grabbed a metal probe. He started scraping my teeth.

"So, the studio says we need to fit you for some fangs. You gonna be a vampire in this movie or something?" I tried to say 'uh uh,' but what came out sounded more like, "Ngah ngah." When he removed the steel pick from my mouth, I told him I was set to play a demon that possesses a small child. Again, he nodded casually. I was starting to get the impression I wasn't the first person he'd fit for special dental effects before. Or, the second person.

He continued to poke around my mouth for a bit, probing and brushing. After a while it started to feel like a regular visit. I realized it *was* a regular visit when he made me aware I could use a little work. He even made a few suggestions as to some things he could do during this visit. Did I take any offense to that assessment? Not really. I knew I'd been putting off a dental checkup for some time. And heck, I wasn't going to argue about having a pretty smile, so I agreed to his suggestions. The dentist must have picked up on my utter fear of dentists since he decided to put me under with laughing gas. I don't know why they called it laughing gas because suddenly I didn't think anything was funny.

Now, I forget exactly *everything* I agreed to, but nonetheless, I *did* agree, and the dentist put me under. When I woke up, I'd had about four days' worth of dental work done in one day. And, he'd also taken the mold of my newly improved pearly whites and made the fangs right there, on the spot. I was delighted. Dental work and special effects, all in one day. I couldn't wait to show off my new smile to Jo. However, shortly before leaving the office, I popped in my fangs and decided to have a little fun on the way home.

As I was walking out of the dentist's office, a young boy and his mother were coming in. I held the door for them. The little boy said, "Thank you." I turned, lowered my head so I was at eye-level with him, smiled wide and said, "You're welcome, hun!" Poor kid nearly bowled his mother over as he flinched hard and fell backward, right into her lap.

I also tried to frighten a bus driver. While I typically walked or rode a bike around the city, on this day, I felt like taking the bus.

I picked one up not far from the dentist's office. As I was walking toward the bus stop, I took a red lipstick out of my purse and smeared my lips a bit. Not too aggressive, but just enough to be noticeable. When I saw the bus, I stepped a bit closer to the curb. The driver pulled up and opened the door. I reached for a few coins and climbed the steps. After I handed him the change, I looked directly at him and asked, "Do you know where I could find a good butcher?"

He stared at me, completely stoic. "Cute," he said. "Take a seat."

I thought to myself, *Oh well, one-for-two ain't bad.*

Not long after I had the fangs made, I had to visit an eye doctor to get fitted for contact lenses. I'd never worn contacts before in my life so I wasn't sure how to put these in or take them out. The thing to keep in mind here is that these lenses were nothing like the "dailies" or "monthlies" that are prescribed today. These were made of a much harder, more solid material. You felt every part of these lenses. Once, when I was trying them on by myself at home, the lenses got stuck. I freaked out. I tried to take them out and the more I messed with them, the more irritated my eyes became. So I waited. Then I tried again. Five minutes of trying and again, I waited. Then tried again. Then waited. It got so bad I started to panic. Jo wasn't home so I couldn't ask her for help. I ran out of my apartment and downstairs where there lived the son of a guy with who I'd worked on a film. I quickly explained to him what happened and he basically told me to calm down, let the irritation in my eyes settle a bit. We doused my eyes with enough saline solution to fill a pint glass. Then he told me to hold my eyes open while he pinched the edges. He said, "This might feel weird." I didn't care. Anything to get them out at this point.

It didn't take him long to remove the lenses from my eyes but, my god, my eyes were red for days.

Spitting Practice

Since the screen tests were over and I still needed some work on my spitting technique, I decided to create a little "homework" for myself. My homework was to find something at home I could hang up and spit at.

I tried spitting in the shower but the problem with this was, I couldn't see where it was going. Fortunately, my apartment had these enormous windows with pull-down shades. I attached a paper bulls-eye to the screen and practiced spitting like a man. I did something like curl my tongue, let it out with a burst of breath. And let me tell you, my aim got *very* good.

The Exorcist: First Day of Shooting in New York

I took one of the only cabs I've ever taken in New York City my first official day on the set. It was six a.m., still dark, and the last thing I wanted to do was walk down Fifty-Fourth Street in darkness. When I arrived, the studio was completely unassuming from the outside. It was a very nondescript brick building. If I was a casual passerby, I would have never known the scariest movie in cinema history was being shot there.

A security guard met me as I walked in. I introduced myself and he allowed me inside. It was a closed set (a "closed set" is when nobody is allowed on the set except for the actors and crew) but I had a call time that day so I was allowed in. Aside from those required to be on set, only the folks from Los Angeles (the people from Warner Brothers) were allowed. It was easy to spot them, they were all tan.

I walked through the set in complete awe. They'd recreated the whole inside of Regan MacNeil's house. There was a bedroom set, living room set, kitchen set, etc., all built inside of a soundstage. It was like no other set I'd ever seen before. Every detail captured, every nuance brought to life; from the counters, to the furnishings, to the window treatments.

It was just like a real house on the inside. It was exactly as I'd pictured the house in my head the first time I read Blatty's book, and it looked magnificent.

After taking a quick look around, I walked to the makeup room. It was a walk that would soon become very familiar to me. I remember my heart beat wildly as I approached the room. I was a little scared. *My first major motion picture*, I thought. I was going to be working with actors like Ellen Burstyn, Max von Sydow, Jason Miller, Lee J. Cobb. I saw the makeup room, walked around the corner and looked inside. The first person I saw was Dick Smith. I went straight to him. He said, "Hi Eileen," gave me a big hug, and all the fear that had boiled up inside me quickly simmered down to a calm. I immediately felt I was home.

The makeup room had four chairs that faced a huge mirror. Bill Farley, the hair stylist, also used the makeup room. This way, someone could sit in the chair waiting for makeup to dry, while Bill did their hair for that day.

Dick told me to find my dressing room in order to get ready for him and his team. I walked out of the room and down the hall toward the dressing rooms. I saw a room that said, "Ellen Burstyn." The next room was, "Linda Blair." The next, "Eileen Dietz." Jason Miller's room was after mine and Max von Sydow's was next to his. I couldn't believe I was right in the middle of all these people. I had my own dressing room!

There was a couch in my room, a little desk with a mirror, a chair and a place to hang up clothes. I'd be lying if I said I wasn't immediately overwhelmed with pride at the fact I had my own dressing room among all these stars. But I didn't want Dick and the others to wait long. So I pulled off my heavy winter coat and boots, and then got changed into what I thought people wore to a makeup room. I put on an old shirt and a pair of jeans. After that, I got myself a black coffee from craft services, headed back into the makeup room, sat down in a chair and was ready to begin.

Demon in the Mirror

People often ask if I ever got scared from seeing myself in the mirror with full demon makeup. I most definitely did. Sometimes I couldn't "find" myself. I had trouble seeing where Eileen ended and Dick Smith's prosthetics began. Beneath all that latex and makeup, I knew I was there somewhere. After a while though, I started to get used to it. Occasionally, if I had to get up to use the bathroom or get something from another room, I would pass a mirror and think, *Oh my God! Is that what I really look like???* So every night when I got home and the makeup was removed, I would look into the mirror again, just to make sure it was me.

I actually spent more time on the set as Pazuzu/Regan than I did as myself. Sometimes, I spent an entire day in makeup, from six a.m. to six p.m., and I wouldn't even get to act. This is pretty common. On film sets actors typically spend more time waiting than they do shooting. This includes the biggest stars down to the Extras. Some actors complain about waiting all day and not working until the end of it, if at all. Not me. I was so happy to be on a set, working with some of the biggest names in the movie business and getting paid for it. I figured they actually paid me to be there not necessarily to act.

The makeup they used was far less than what was originally conceived. In our makeup tests we had huge bushy eyebrows, big fangs and really wild hair. Dick Smith decided to remove a lot of it since we looked too much like monsters. He wanted Linda and me to still be recognizable as Regan. He thought the eyebrows, fangs, and big hair were far too over-the-top; like a stereotypical devil.

Dick used scars and scratches along with the prosthetics to make our faces look swollen. He used all purples, blues, and yellows to indicate bruising. Dick and Billy wanted Regan to look like a little girl who'd been terribly beaten in a fight. And she was. She'd been in a fight with the Devil himself.

The scratches/prosthetics were formed so as to contour to the life-masks Dick had made of both Linda and I. Then, pieces of rubber were glued to my face with special glue. This took some time because each piece had to be applied individually. Then it had to dry. *Then* they would apply the next piece, and so on.

The next thing Dick did was color the prosthetics with a flesh tone. This required a lot of different colors and a lot of time was spent making sure the mixture was accurate. Once that was dry, Dick literally painted on the blood around the scratches. Just like a true artist, he used a pallet full of deep reds, purples, and blacks to turn Regan into a demon. My nose was also taped up a bit to look like Linda's. Then the wig went on and three-and-a-half hours after we started, I was done.

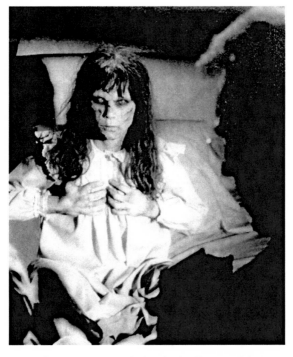

Me and Max von Sydow in the Foreground

Regan Look

It was a very long and intense process, but the results made it appear as if it was all very simple. I think that's what made it so scary to me. When I saw the screen tests of me and Linda in the original makeup, it was clearly overdone and hardly scary. But in the final makeup, it was kind of terrifying. On one hand, I knew it was me staring back at myself in the mirror. But on the other hand, Dick really created an entirely different person. When we were done filming for the day and it was time to take the makeup off, I was back in the chair for at least another hour. Each prosthetic had to be removed separately. The makeup assistant would use a clean brush, dip it into a solvent, brush it underneath a piece of rubber, and gently pull it off my face. Unfortunately, we couldn't just pull the stuff off like band-aids--I wanted to. Each piece had to be removed just as it had gone on--individually. It required far more patience to sit in the chair with the solvent running down my face than it did to have my demon face put on every morning. Many times an assistant would heat up a towel and lay it over my face once all the makeup was removed. That was bliss.

I loved it all and I never got restless. I never felt antsy, like I had to get out of the makeup chair. Even to this day, I still find the process relaxing. For someone who talks a lot and is often up and down, once I sit in a makeup chair, which always seems to be three-and-a-half hours, I relax and go into a kind of a meditation. I loved sitting in the chair, watching great stars like Ellen Burstyn and Max Von Sydow come into the room. The time spent in the chair was really my opportunity to take it all in, to immerse myself in the experience. However, I would often treat myself to facials so I could see a young, scrubbed face staring at myself in the mirror. The irony here is, this kind of pampering often led to some pain.

As good as that solvent is for your face, you tend to forget you've been covered in makeup for hours (Sometimes an entire day!). Once the makeup is gone and your face is clean again, your pores are so open and your skin is so sensitive, it absorbs just about anything. One time, after we had wrapped for the day, I made the mistake of going to the movies and eating popcorn. Imagine a pair of salty-fingered hands touching your face after a day like that. I don't have to imagine it because I *did* it. It felt like little grains of fire burning all the way down into the middle of my face. It gave me a greater appreciation for the expression, "rubbing salt on the wound."

I enjoyed the time spent in the makeup chair, all those long hours with Linda and Dick. Someone had this great idea to set up a TV behind Linda and me so we could watch our shows through the mirror in front of us. Of course everything was backwards but that didn't matter. Generally the TV was only on in the mornings. Linda preferred to watch reruns of *I Love Lucy*. I preferred the morning news. This sometimes led to arguments, but we actually got along a lot better than most people think. We became friends during filming. We spent a lot of time in her dressing room playing games and talking about all kinds of things. On the days she had to be tutored and wouldn't be on the set, I would feel lonely. But I would remember I was there to do a job and got over it.

Therapist Ball-Grab

The day we shot the scene where Regan is with the psychiatrist, played by Arthur Storch, Linda and I didn't require much makeup. In the scene the psychiatrist tries to speak with the demon and tries to draw it out. After several attempts there's an on-screen transformation where, finally, the demon shows itself. That's when I make my first appearance.

On "Action!", I had to leap from the chair, grab Storch's testicles, rendering him helpless and in pain, then fall to the floor. At least, that's how Friedkin had explained it to me. And he wanted me to go for it. I mean, *really* go for it, grab him *hard.* Now, nobody ever told me anything about an athletic supporter. Even if someone had said, "Don't worry, Arthur is wearing a cup," I wouldn't have known what that was. I didn't grow up with any brothers and I'd never been introduced to such "personal protection" before. So I assumed I was going to grab the real thing. It seemed a bit awkward to me but I thought, *Oh well, Storch is a professional. I'm sure it will hurt, but he'll be okay with it. It'll be good for the movie.*

After Grabbing Arthur Storch's Balls

So, Friedkin calls "Action!" I jump from the chair, reach for Storch's crotch and I grab onto something VERY hard. It shocked the hell out of me. I thought, *What the hell did I just grab?* I almost broke character. Also, I would be lying if I said the thought hadn't crossed my mind that Storch was umm…"aroused." After the first take, someone on the set had told me Storch was wearing a cup. When he explained to me what a cup was, it made a *lot* more sense. It also made things less weird when we shot the next take.

Smacking Ellen Burstyn

Something about smacking a world-renowned actress like Ellen Burstyn seemed kind of surreal to me (as if shooting a movie made up like a demon-possessed little girl wasn't surreal enough). Who the hell was I, Eileen Dietz, to be smacking around *any* actor, never mind one of the best in the business? It's the scene during which Chris MacNeil and Father Karras are standing in the hallway when they hear Regan crying out for help (along with other loud, strange noises). When they rush into Regan's bedroom I get up on my knees and smack Ellen so hard she falls and rolls to the other side of the room.

When Bill explained to me what my role was, it seemed simple and harmless. I wasn't going to be delivering a knock-out blow by any stretch of the imagination. Ellen wore a harness during the scene which was to be yanked back by a grip, sitting off-camera. My role was simply to swing my hand past her face, as if slapping her, then the grip would pull her down to the ground, showing Regan's otherworldly (i.e. demonic) powers.

After the first take, I could tell immediately Ellen was surprised by how much force the grip used when he pulled her down. She even mentioned to Billy she felt she was going to get hurt. Bill acknowledged her concern. Perhaps a bit dismissively. I remember seeing an exchange between Bill and the grip afterward, as if he had said, "pull her HARD." In reading subsequent interviews with Ellen, I realized she'd noticed the same exchange. But, we rolled again.

The second time was when she got hurt. She screamed in pain, just like she was supposed to, but it was real pain. That scene ended up permanently damaging her spine. She can walk, sure, but I know she still has pain in that area to this day.

Another trick they employed during this scene involved the use of a gun. As Father Karras, Chris MacNeil and Chris' assistant, Sharon Spencer, enter the room, Friedkin wanted their reaction to a possessed Regan to be as real and terrifying as possible. So as they entered the room, a gun was fired somewhere nearby. None of the actors knew this was coming. Reactions ranged from surprise to fear to shock to even tears. That was just for Take One. On Take Two, the gun went off again. This time the actors were only mildly shocked. On Take Three, it started to become annoying and people began to wonder what the hell was going on.

The Special Effects crew also tried to get natural reactions by provoking other senses; one of them being the sense of smell. They decided a demon probably smells really bad so, without telling anyone, they'd mixed together a nasty concoction of raw rotten meat and rotten eggs with other any vile thing they could get their hands on. When the demon was to make an appearance during a particular scene, they'd bring out this mixture. The smell was so bad we had to stop shooting because members of the crew literally got sick and we would have to wait while they ran to the bathroom to throw up. They only tried that once.

Soup's On!

For a lot of people who have seen the movie, green pea soup has never looked the same since *The Exorcist* was released in 1973. I'm referring to the famous green-pea vomit scene. I'm still in awe of what Billy Friedkin and Dick Smith were able to accomplish.

Dick had built a contraption involving a tube inserted under the makeup on my face and continued inside my mouth. The appliance was originally designed so the cameraman would only be able to shoot one side of my face. When Billy saw it, he said it wouldn't work; he needed to shoot both sides of my face. So Dick redesigned the contraption so there were two tubes--

one on either side of my face--and those tubes would again converge in my mouth and projectile-shoot the green pea soup at Fathers Merrin and Karras.

Dick then used additional prosthetics and makeup to hide the tubes. The tubes ran under the bed and off-set and were connected to a pump. On "Action," a special effects guy would pump the stuff through the tubes, into my mouth and, ultimately, all over the actors. Fortunately, this didn't require many takes, but it did take a while to reset after each shot. I also had to change my nightgown several times. Not that I ever minded, but I was a smoker at the time and would have given anything for a cigarette or for something to eat. I also couldn't talk much. As it was, I wasn't able to do either until the shot was finished.

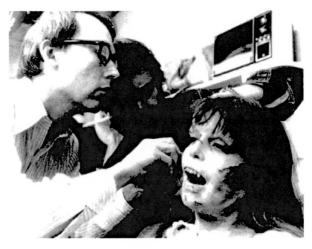

Dick Smith Applying Vomit Appliance

In order to make the shoot a bit easier on me, Dick created a spit sucker, which is very similar to what a dentist uses to suck the saliva out of a patient's mouth. He attached a small tube to something that looked like a vacuum cleaner and *whoosh*, it soaked up the saliva gathered in my mouth.

Vomit Scene

Jason Miller, who played Father Karras, was more than willing to take some green-pea soup in the face; however, I don't think he ever quite understood *how* much soup was going to come out. In fact, I'm not sure any of us knew. Jason was not pleased when the pea soup hit him in the face, but it certainly worked for the scene. I understood that later, the editors enhanced the flow of the vomit so it would look more direct

151

but this didn't concern me. The scene certainly was memorable and when people talk about *The Exorcist*, this is one of the first scenes they mention. I myself have never eaten pea soup again. Fun fact: The filmmakers chose Andersen's green pea soup over Campbell's as Andersen's better achieved the effect they needed.

Who Turned on the A/C?

One of the big things that made the experience challenging was the cold. They basically built a freezer around the entire bedroom set. They had these enormous air conditioning units that ran from floor to ceiling. Every night, they'd turn on the ACs so, by the next day, the set was cooled to somewhere around ten degrees. It was literally freezing. The idea was that when the demon is present, the entire room would go cold. And, in order to show how cold it was, it was necessary to see people's breath. Friedkin, Owen Rozman (the Cinematographer), and most of the crew wore wet suits when the room was that cold. Max Von Sydow and Jason Miller wore wet suits under their priest robes. Linda and I wore only our nightgowns.

At one point, someone had the idea that if people ate food, we'd be able to stay warm. Outside the set there was a stand that cooked hotdogs, hamburgers, soups, chili, etc. After a while, people started gaining weight. I never ate that food because I was still so concerned with keeping my twelve year-old figure. And who could really be hungry shooting the possession scenes or eating with the prosthetics in place? In fact, I didn't eat much throughout the shoot. I had other things on my mind. Often it was so cold in the room our eyes would tear up and we wondered if we could stand it anymore, but of course we persevered. Fortunately for me, most of the time I was under the covers.

Levitation Scene

The levitation scene made me nervous. I was called to the set a bit earlier than needed so I could watch Linda do the scene first. It was simple but intricate. Linda laid down in a clear, hard plastic cradle. It was hoisted by wires that were attached on the opposite end to a crank. The idea was to show a slowly levitating Regan, lifted by the power of...Satan? God? In the finished film, the cradle and wires were never seen.

What made me nervous was the cradle being incredibly small. I'm a small woman, but this thing was dangerously small. But it had to be in order to make it easier to hide on camera.

When it came time for me to do the scene, I laid down and stayed very still. I prayed to myself that the guy operating the crank had had enough coffee throughout the day and he wouldn't let the thing slip and drop me. Either way, the worst-case scenario likely would have been I'd simply fall onto the bed.

But they lifted me so *high*! It didn't look that high when Linda was in the cradle. When I was finally lifted, I swore I was ten feet off the ground and pretty damn close to the ceiling.

Then Friedkin called cut and the crank operator lowered me slowly back down to the bed. This action was repeated often during the days we shot. At first, the idea of being lifted so high off the ground in this tiny plastic device, while Merrin and Karras shouted incantations at the demon inside Regan, was a harrowing one. It was also freezing up there, at the top of the set. It seemed the air conditioning whooshed under the nightgown to Linda and my very toes. And we couldn't wear long johns to stay warm because our legs were exposed. *But*, by the time we did the last shot it was just plain fun being lifted in the air and floating.

The Abuse of the Cross Scene

At last it was time to shoot the infamous crucifix-masturbation scene. This was the primary reason I'd been hired to do the film. It would have been terribly inappropriate (and probably illegal) for a twelve-year-old Linda to perform the scene. Even by my own standards, as accustomed as I had become to shooting unusual things, this was really weird.

I wore underwear during the shot. Over my underwear I wore a sponge filled with fake blood. When I brought the crucifix down, it went straight into the sponge spraying "blood" everywhere. Billy and I discussed what he wanted from the shot. Actually, it was one of the few times he ever spoke directly to me. And although they would cut straight to Linda's face in the finished film, he needed a reaction of desire and fulfillment. I guess what he meant was some kind of climax. I remember thinking, *Wow, this is getting really serious.*

Then he sat down on the bed and proceeded to show me how to "insert" the crucifix into the sponge. He put his fingers around the crucifix and proceeded to move it up and down in a jerky movement. I first thought, *No, this isn't going to work. My hand isn't at the right angle. I need to tip my wrist.*

Now, it was only me and a small group of men on the set during this shoot. Among the men were Owen Rozman, some grips, a few electrics, Marcel (the special effects guy), a set photographer, and Billy. So I was much too shy to say, "I think this is how it must be done. Like a girl," even though the demon was definitely a male. So I just sat there moving my hand in what I thought was the proper position, jabbing upward. That's when Billy said, "No, *this* is how I want you to do it." And he made the proper motions with the crucifix.

He started showing me and everyone else who was in the room how it was done. It was a little awkward to say the least. Then Billy noticed the set photographer taking pictures of him, "jerking off." That's when he jumped off the bed, grabbed the camera, and just like in a movie, opened it up and ripped all

155

the film out--crumbling it up in his hand and throwing it on the floor. No one said a word. Then Billy closed the set. It was now just me, Owen the Cinematographer, the guy who marked the shot, and the prop guy. Ultimately, Friedkin decided any film the set photographer shot would have to go through him and we were forbidden to take pictures on the set. Even Dick Smith only managed to grab a few shots.

The Original Cross Used in Masturbation Scene

The scene was gross and fun at the same time. We did a lot of takes. I had the crucifix at the correct angle with blood all over my thighs and hands and even had some good sounds and groans and sighs. I had a lot of fun with it but had no idea at the time how the scene would affect everyone who saw it. I took to calling it, "The abuse of the cross sequence."

Death Scene

As much as we had rehearsed the Death scene, I was not prepared for the performance Jason Miller delivered. To this day, it is equally one of the most brilliant *and* haunting moments of the film, for me.

Prior to shooting the scene, we blocked out our movements. "Blocking" refers to how you move around and through a scene as you read your lines (either Billy or the first director would tell us where to move, moment by moment, as the scene unfolded). The director will give you cues as to when and where you're supposed to be, prior to shooting the scene. It's like this beautifully orchestrated series of movements that, when finished, looks like a completely fluid and seemingly natural flow of a given scene. Basically, it's how the "magic" happens. On *The Exorcist*, blocking was even choreographed by the numbers, like:

1: Jason sees Max.

2: Jason looks at Eileen.

3: Jason lunges for the bed…and so forth.

It was all set up to be a very simple, easy wrestling scene. I, as Regan, am sitting on the bed. Father Merrin has just had a heart attack. Father Karras comes into the room, sees Merrin lying unconscious and tries to revive him. Karras then looks at Regan. I giggle. Karras rushes over to the bed, wrestles me off and we fall to the floor. Jason was to basically cradle me somewhat so I didn't get hurt as we crashed to the floor. Then, we would tousle on the floor a bit more, stare at each other, Regan's eyes would close, Karras' eyes would then change, showing the manifestation of the demon now inside him, and we'd cut. Then they'd bring in Linda and shoot the big finale where Karras is shown jumping through the window. It was all supposed to be so harmless.

So we get into our positions. I'm on the bed, Jason is standing by the bedpost. Friedkin yells, "Action!" Miller runs to Von Sydow, sees Father Merrin is dead. That's when he looks at me and suddenly, I don't see Jason. I see a rabid German Shepherd, a deranged beast ready to kill me. He grabs me by both arms, throws me to the floor (no gentle tousling on the bed. Blocking and "by the numbers" went out the window). I'm thinking the man was ready to choke me. Friedkin then yells cut and it's over.

I felt a bit dazed and checked my arms and legs to make sure they were all right. I was fine. I thought we were done, too, but I was wrong--that was only the first take. Miller immediately apologized, which was completely unnecessary. I was surprised, but glad he went for it. Jason Miller had never been known for his acting--he was Pulitzer Prize-winning playwright. I hadn't expected him to turn into such a monster, but he was fantastic.

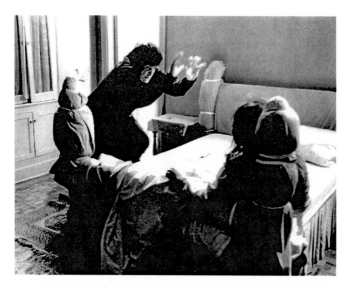

Death Scene with Jason Miller

We ended up doing several takes ("takes" are how many times the director chooses to shoot a scene. Sometimes it will only be one take, other times it can be 20 or more, depending on the director). Neither Jason nor I were stunt people. We didn't have knee pads or elbow pads or any kind of protection like stunt people wear. All I had on was my nightgown and all he wore was his priest robes. We both ended up with some heavy bruising after we shot that scene, but it was all worth it.

It looked great on film. And, it was after shooting this scene when I ultimately decided I would *never* do stunt work. You've gotta be both nuts and highly trained. I was lucky I didn't get hurt. Ironically, one of the stunt men who worked on the film (the one who went out the window and onto the now-famous Georgetown steps where Father Karras dies) must have liked what he saw in me because he asked if I was interested in doing stunt work full time. I politely turned him down. I still have friends who love to call me from those same steps in Georgetown and say "Hey, guess where I am!" They are *that* famous.

CHAPTER NINE

Strange Goings-On

There are a lot of stories that came out of the filming of *The Exorcist*. Many have been recorded and reported before. When asked if I personally recall anything strange that happened, either during the filming, or perhaps as a result of the movie, there are a few things that come to mind.

There are reported to be about fourteen things that happened during filming, including several deaths. Ironically, the film took fourteen months to shoot. And surely life happens and people die in that amount of time, but the facts are there. The actor who played Burke Dennings--Jack MacGowran--died before the movie was released. I can only add what I saw and what happened to me.

A priest was on hand to bless the set just about every day. He would bless the living room set, then the kitchen and then the bedroom so all was covered. He would come down to the set where the whole crew was setting up for the day's shoot. There was the usual noise of people running around to get things ready. There were conversations about the night before, perhaps something on TV, something about the kids, the traffic getting to the set...but when the priest came down, a hush would fall over the entire crew. Everyone stopped what they were doing and either listened, bowed or prayed.

I don't know if this was Billy's idea, or if someone was concerned with fooling around with the devil, but the notion of a priest blessing the set served as great publicity. Once the public found out a priest was visiting the set each day, the buzz around the film was palpable. Imagine: a horror film being made was considered *so* scary, the filmmakers had to bring a priest on the set every day to make sure it was blessed so everybody felt safe.

It was also a closed set--absolutely no one was allowed to visit or to watch. Everything was top-secret and the only visitors I saw where the men who came in with suits and suntans. They were checking on the progress of the film which, by now, was way over budget and over time. We heard every time the "tanned guys" came to visit, Billy lost points on the movie ("Points" are part of the back-end of a film--the amount of money you get after the film shows a profit. One point on a film like *The Exorcist* came to be worth a whole lot of money).

The way I understood it, Billy didn't care. He was going to make this film his way. And he did. One of the reasons we were so far behind is Billy would take one look at a finished set, tell the crew he hated it, then force them to rebuild a whole new set and the rest of us would all go on a long hiatus (that is, a *paid* hiatus). We were all on contract so we couldn't go anywhere, much less work on another project, so we sat and waited for the next work call to come in. It would end up being a very big unemployment check.

My sister Deni had a miscarriage while I was filming *The Exorcist.* It didn't happen when most miscarriages happen, not one at six or eight weeks. When she miscarried, she miscarried a half-formed baby. It was horribly sad. And although it could happen to anyone, it didn't happen to just anyone. It happened to the sister of the actress who was playing a demon in a film about God, the Devil, and exorcism.

Another thing that made me start believing in the Spirit world happened when I was being dressed in my wardrobe. I was in the green nightgown and nothing else but panties, waiting to be called to the set. And I don't know why it happened that day but I suddenly thought, *It's just too cold on that set. I don't think I can do this today. I just can't be that cold.* And with that thought, the entire sprinkler system went off and started to drench the set. It took some time to turn off the sprinklers but they finally did. Unfortunately, the damage had already been done and they had to open the huge double doors that led on and off the set. The doors rolled up and the sun came in. As unfortunate as the sprinkler delay was, the sun was a welcomed surprise. When you are shooting a film on a sound stage you

163

live in a blackened world day in and day out. And if you're shooting during the winter months, like we were, you come to work in the dark and you go home in the dark.

They had to turn off the air conditioners and let the whole place dry out. We also had to continue shooting. We couldn't lose another day, but it also would have taken all night to bring the temperature down. So, my "prayers" were answered and it was warm. If you watch one of the scenes in the movie with Regan and Father Merrin, you will notice for a few frames there is no vapor coming from our mouths. And now you know why.

Aside from all the creepy and spooky things that happened, there really wasn't a lot of humor on the set. At least not when I was there. I think it's because Friedkin ran such a tight ship, that the crew didn't have time to joke around and keep things loose. However, someone pulled a good one on me I'll never forget. I was in the makeup room. Dick had already started to apply some prosthetics to my face and neck and I had to pee. I decided it was probably better I go now than wait and have to go afterward, when the makeup is done and they need to shoot my scene.

So I trudged into the bathroom in my gown, half my makeup on and half asleep (it was very early in the morning), and as I entered the stall, I nearly had a heart attack when I saw an arm sticking out of the toilet--hand and fingers open and reaching outward. I nearly fell over as I screamed and jumped backward out of the stall, crashing through the door. I was ready to bolt out of the room right then and there when I saw Bill Farley, his assistant, and the Alan Green, standing by the sinks, laughing their assess off. At that point, I couldn't help but bust out in laughter, too. After a while, I couldn't tell if they were still laughing at my reaction to the arm in the toilet, or if they were now laughing at my appearance as my half-applied makeup was now dangling from my face.

Alan Green, along with the First AD, Terry Donnelly, knew how tough some of the possession scenes were and whenever I needed help getting on or off the bed, strapping into the levitation cradle, or cleaning up after a vomit take, they always did their best to make me as comfortable as possible; either with an easy gesture or a sympathetic smile.

The Making of the Icon Known as Captain Howdy

One day I was called into the makeup room and Dick told me we were going to shoot another character--Pazuzu's face--alone, when he wasn't inside the body of Regan. He told me they had been working on various makeup tests, one of which was a black-and-white face with red eyes and "outrageous teeth." I wish I knew exactly how it happened but there is no one to ask. There is Dick Smith. And although I have been privileged to meet Dick for lunch a couple of times with his amazing friend Jill (who brought him from Connecticut to Los Angeles to retire), we have never discussed *The Exorcist* in particular; only his amazing career.

It was decided they would use this image over the face of Father Karras' mother during Karras' dream sequence, as his mother comes out of the subway. It was a fairly simple makeup compared to that of Regan's but still, only an artist could've made it work. I and others have tried to duplicate it for Halloween or parties and it is just elusive. Dick was not only an artist, he was an innovator and came up with makeup ideas on *The Exorcist* that had never been tried before; such as the mechanism in the dummy Regan that made the head turn around 360 degrees. I'll never forget the morning I walked into the makeup room and saw "Regan" sitting in the chair next to mine. I walked in, set my things down on the counter by the mirror, said hello to Dick and then I turned to what I thought was Linda sitting there and said, "Hi Linda. How are you doing?" After a few seconds of no response, I took a closer look and realized I'd just talked to the dummy. I then looked at Dick who gave me a wink, as if to say, "Gotcha," and then got into my chair and waited for Dick to finish applying some makeup to dummy-Regan.

We shot the set-ups with this makeup from many different angles and it was a New York Studio wrap of the film. The shot they used was almost subliminal. If you weren't totally focused you would've missed it. But in its own way, this contributed to the magic and mystery of the film. Of course when the film opened in 1973, there were no VCRs much less DVDs or home videotape. So people would see the film and after it was over, one would say to another, "Hey, did you see that face?" "What face?" "The one on Father Karras' mother when she came out of the subway." So they would go back and see the film time after time just to see the face that became known as "The Face of Death." In The Version You Have Never Seen Before, the face is seen more often (four times), but the horror remains.

Regan the Dummy

In the beginning of the film, Chris MacNeil hears some voices coming out of the basement playroom. When she goes to investigate she sees Regan playing with a Ouija Board. Chris asks her to whom she is talking. Regan looks up and says, "Captain Howdy." Thus, The Face of Death was given a name. Kids tried to stop their VHS tapes to pause on the face and have since found it much easier to pause on a DVD.

Captain Howdy

I have been told by fans it is The Face of Death that still gives them nightmares after all these years; that this face was the most frightening part of the film. It is considered by many to be the icon of the film. Fans often tell me they thought it was a man but it's my eyes that give me away. I am fascinated and awed by all of this. I am humbled even more so at how such a simple idea, a "What have we got to lose?" notion has had this kind of lasting effect on people.

Unfortunately, and as much fun as we were all having making this film, all good things must come to an end. In the case of *The Exorcist*, being over time and over budget, it started to feel like "the end" was more of a mirage and less of a certainty.

This is *The Exorcist!*

The Exorcist was a long shoot--fourteen months to be exact (ten months of filming, four months of editing). Actors and crews, and especially the office people (the secretaries and production people) are like gypsies. Even though the money was great, it was time to move on. In fact, we used to have a pool as to whether we would work past the next person's birthday. That went along with how many times we would reshoot a scene the next day. Billy was a perfectionist and if he didn't like the dailies (scenes that were already shot and to be reviewed), we would reshoot. He knew what he wanted and that was his way.

As much fun as we were all having, we kept thinking, *it must be coming to an end! It must be ready to wrap!* It wasn't that anyone was tired or bored of the film, but many of us were receiving offers to do other projects so it was difficult to make any commitments without knowing, for sure, when the shoot would end.

The "not knowing" really caught up with me. I was approached about a few different projects, one of which being a play written by Arthur Laurents, the playwright most famous for West Side Story.

The show was scheduled to open in Washington, D.C. and after the run, it would reopen in New York City. I couldn't believe I was going to work with the great Arthur Laurents! To appear on Broadway! Every New York actor's dream! I ran over to the production office to tell them my news. Much to my chagrin, they said no. They said they had no idea when we were going to wrap. "It might be a week or two or three," the line producer told me. I thought, *Oh well, this is The Exorcist,* so I had to turn it down. However, I did end up auditioning for a bank commercial. Much to my delight, I got that gig too.

The commercial was set to shoot about a week after *The Exorcist* was scheduled to wrap. So I gratefully and enthusiastically accepted the job (the neat thing about shooting a commercial is you will collect residuals sometimes for years after you shoot it. And every thirteen weeks it starts up again).

So I was looking forward to a week off between jobs. Then *The Exorcist* shot right past the scheduled end date. No kidding. One day became two; two became three. Suddenly, we were a week over and it was the day before I was scheduled to shoot the commercial. I went to David Salven, the Unit Production Manager, and sheepishly told him I had to be in New Jersey for a commercial the next day. He barked at me. "This is *The Exorcist!* You're signed on to do *this* movie! If you don't show up, you'll be reported to the Screen Actors Guild!" Not wanting to be in any bad standing with SAG, I promptly called the folks making the commercial and told them I couldn't make it. They told me, "You're signed on to do this commercial! If you don't show up, we're going to report you to the Screen Actors Guild!" I suddenly began mulling over that saying about a rock and a hard place.

The commercial was scheduled to shoot two spots--one in the morning and one in the afternoon. I offered to show up in the afternoon and they went for it. All I had to do now was work on the guys back on the film set. News like this travels fast on the set of a movie, so the crew pretty much knew what was going on. Luckily, they helped me out.

The crew on *The Exorcist* generally didn't rush through their work. Nobody seemed to care how many setups were done in a given day, which was probably part of the reason why the film was so over time. They would maybe get through two setups each morning.

The day the commercial was scheduled to shoot was also the day the film was finally set to wrap (again). Word had gotten out I had to be done by noon. The crew put in this herculean effort and we actually shot six setups by noon. When we finished, I and the film were finally wrapped. I was so gratified.

Now I just had to get to New Jersey by lunch. A production assistant grabbed my hand and dragged me to the sink in the makeup room and they washed my face. Captain Howdy didn't have prosthetics, so it was relatively easy to remove. I guess it took about a half hour to get all the black and white makeup off. Next it was off to another chair where they pulled off the hair band and washed my hair. They even gave me a light makeup. The production assistant was like a mother hen, leading me from place to place. I finally changed my clothes and they had a limo waiting for me downstairs in the alley. As luck would have it, I made it to the set of the bank commercial by lunch time.

I don't remember much about the commercial except that it said something about having a "jingle in my pocket." And I sure did get a piece of that jingle. The commercial ran for two years and netted me a nice chunk of change. I certainly dodged a bullet, thanks to a wonderful crew who, I assume, really liked me.

Kitty Winn (who played Sharon Spencer, the on-screen assistant to Burstyn's Chris MacNeil) also encountered similar problems with the no-end-in-sight issue. In exploring other opportunities, Kitty landed an audition for *The Glass Menagerie*, with Katherine Hepburn. The folks from *Glass Menagerie* wanted her so badly they agreed to hold all the rehearsals in New York, for Kitty's convenience. However, because the movie was to be shot in London, she was unable to leave *The Exorcist*. I felt terribly for her. She was a tremendous actress. She'd won a Golden Globe for her role opposite Al Pacino in, *The Panic in Needle Park*. I would have loved to have seen her in *The Glass Menagerie*. Her role in *The Exorcist* was just about done anyway, but they wouldn't let her go. To top it off, Friedkin ended up removing a bunch of her scenes from the final cut. Kitty's character was initially supposed to serve as somewhat of a spiritual intermediary (much like in Blatty's book), between the two extremes of the Church (i.e. God) and the demon. But, Friedkin believed that those scenes might take away from the impact of the possession scenes.

Being a part of the most influential horror film of all time feels amazing, to say the least. Some say it's the scariest movie of all time. I'd have to agree. Given what we were up against and considering the fact we did not have the advantages afforded to filmmakers today (i.e. CGI, computer editing, etc.), it was quite a feat. Billy Friedkin, Dick Smith, Linda, Ellen, Max,

Jason, Lee…they were all the right pieces that fit magically into the same, masterfully-created puzzle.

Of course, none of us ever knew the film would become what it has. At the time, we were all just having fun making a horror movie. I've never forgotten how special it is to have been, and still *be*, a part of it.

CHAPTER TEN

Fan Mail

From time to time, I get letters from people who've seen the movie. They talk about the impact it had on them when they first saw it, as well as the impact the film continues to have on them. Some letters are about my role, specifically, others are about the film as a whole. Some are funny, some like to gush, while others are simply terrifying. I've always been very appreciative of the fans of *The Exorcist* and of their passion for the movie and of the genre. So, here are a few of my favorite fan letters. Enjoy.

Eileen,

I am a bit embarrassed to say I did not know who played "Capt. Howdy" all these years, but now-- just moments ago, as I spilled my green tea on my lap in surprise--I find it is you. How such an enchantingly beautiful woman could become the singular demon that nearly scared me out of the house when I watched *The Exorcist* all those years ago is something I do not know how to explain. It just seems impossible, and yet I see it is not an internet hoax, and I suppose I'm the millionth person to express the same to you.

Cheers from Texas,

Danel

Dear Eileen,

The Exorcist is one film that was never allowed in my grandma's house. Every time I tried to watch it she would forbid it and start praying. I never knew exactly what she was talking about until I snuck it into the house one day. I watched it and must say the film was intense. It was intense because knowing someone can be possessed by a demon was hard to take in. That movie was the reason why I started researching demons and exorcisms and I'll tell you one thing, I have stayed away, and probably always will stay away, from Ouija boards.

Reyna

Eileen,

When I was young, my mother had us watch *The Exorcist*. It stills scares the hell out of me. We were devout Catholics at the time. I would sit there in my bed at night, for many nights over the years, and hold my eyes shut very tight because I knew if I opened them, *she* (Pazuzu) would be sitting on the end of my bed waiting for me.

Harry

Dear Eileen,

I think I was about eight or nine when I first saw *The Exorcist* and if memory serves, I saw it on Starcase or HBO back in the early days of cable television. I don't think I've ever slept quite as soundly since that time. You should be very proud of your contributions to the film. "Captain Howdy" has become a mainstay in the genre of horror. When people think of the horror that is *The Exorcist*, it is your visage that has subliminally shocked the world. It's somewhat comforting to know it is only the "very approachable" Eileen Dietz behind the makeup. But only a little...Best wishes to you and thanks for the screams!

Sincerely,

Michael

Eileen,

I was twenty-three years old when a co-worker of mine told me *The Exorcist* was a movie I had to see at least once within my lifetime. He brought me his own personal copy and loaned it to me. This particular copy happened to be the "Version You've Never Seen," re-released with the spider-walk scene intact and the somewhat subliminal flashes of the Face of Death, so my very first viewing of the scariest movie ever made was going to be 110 percent no holds barred. It was one of those October nights where the wind was howling and a storm was trying to decide whether or not it wanted to blow through. I remember telling myself, "It's kind of creepy, but not too bad." Then the infamous spider-walk scene happened and it was one of those WTF moments. I nearly had a heart attack when the Face of Death flashed on screen. I can tell you with no exaggeration that I was ready to turn it off, but watched on. About midway through the movie, the power decides it wants to go out. It took several minutes for me to work up the nerve to go to the garage and check the circuit breakers. It wasn't long before the power came back on and I finished the film.

A few years later I found out I'd be meeting Eileen Dietz at a horror convention so I bought the DVD for her to sign. I figured it would be okay. I'd never have to watch the thing right? Wrong again! Something inside me made me watch *The Exorcist* for a second time and this is why it has become my favorite scary movie; even after seeing it once already and knowing what I was in for, this film still had the ability to scare me just as badly as it did the first time I saw it. To date I have only been able to watch *The Exorcist* five times and every time I have nightmares and sleep with every light on in the house. Even after meeting Eileen and seeing how nice and lovely a person she is, Captain Howdy/Pazuzu/Face of Death still scares the hell out of me (sorry to be cliché). But, scared or not I will always cherish my *Exorcist* DVD and rank it among my most precious possessions. And whenever somebody asks me what's the scariest movie I have ever seen, the answer will always be, *The Exorcist*.

Lenny

Eileen,

I have three older sisters who made me go see *The Exorcist*. I didn't want to go because I heard people were throwing up in the theaters. We went to the drive-in to see it and I sat in the back seat. I would barely open my eyes to look but I could hear the demon voice so I would open the back door and lean out like I was going to get sick, but of course nothing came out. It was just the fear of hearing and seeing a possessed girl. Of course, after so many times my sisters either got tired of me doing it or they actually felt sorry for me (I was only in elementary school). We left before it was over.

Take care,

Liz

The first time I saw *The Exorcist* was in a packed theater in Singapore, in English, with Mandarin subtitles. I went to see it by myself because my parents either couldn't or wouldn't see it with me. I was entranced by it and cannot remember uttering a word, or making a sound throughout the entire film. I remember other people gasping, and making various noises here and there, but I was silent, completely engrossed by the spectacle--an equal participant and observer to a kind of mass supernatural experience. Throughout the years, I have searched for behind-the-scenes material to try and figure out why the film frightened me and so many others. I have come to the conclusion it is not an issue with Faith or with Science; it is what I don't *want* to see when I view *The Exorcist*. It is the flashes of that white face with the demonic eyes and rotting teeth.

THAT is what most frightens me when I see the film.

Sincerely,

Joaquin

One day I was watching a movie I had taped called *Terror in the Aisles,* which was a compilation of the scariest scenes from horror films from the Seventies and Eighties. One of the movies excerpted was *The Exorcist,* which I had not yet seen. I knew about the film's reputation, and grew up in a religious home so the movie was even more frightening to me since it seemed like something that could actually happen. Even though I was scared, I was fascinated and continued to watch the movie. For a split second, a face flashed on the screen that did not look anything like Regan McNeil, who was scary enough on her own. It was gone before I could figure out what it was. I whipped out the remote control and ran it back and forth, trying to figure out what exactly the image was and how it fit with the rest of what I saw. I decided I had seen some kind of secret image viewers weren't supposed to see, maybe something that had been imprinted on the film, like some kind of evil Seal of Approval. I didn't learn the real story behind the image until a few years later. The movie still scares me to the point where I don't really enjoy watching it all that much compared to other horror films, but I still have fond memories of being a kid staring at the television running the tape back and forth and thinking I had stumbled onto a sinister secret!

Best of luck!

Joel

I didn't watch the film in full until I was in my early twenties. My wife Crystal (also a first-time viewer of the movie) and I sat with eyes wide open and with full attention on the screen. After we watched it, I began to think about it. I was thinking about how well-crafted it was, and how almost every performance in the film was near perfect, and how wonderful the effects were, and of the story itself. So I decided to watch it again. While it is a terrifying film, it's also a movie of great beauty and pathos. The priests in the film don't go into that accursed bedroom to deal with that repugnant creature for money, or for glory--they go because that sweet little girl needs help. They both wind up giving literally everything they have for her, laying down their lives to rid the world (and that family) of an unholy evil. That, to me, is really what the movie is about. I count myself as a Christian, which may or may not make me more susceptible to being intrigued by the film. I don't know for sure; I'm not a giant fan of religious horror per se. But in thinking about the film, and whether God himself would approve of it despite the tough imagery, I am struck by what the real priest who was on the set of *The Exorcist* reportedly told the filmmakers and cast: "You are mirroring the creativity of God." I don't know if that really happened or if it's just another *Exorcist* set urban legend, but I think it's a very wise statement.

-Paul

The Exorcist is one of my ten favorite movies and had a major impact on my formative movie-loving years. It continues to inform creative projects I work on to this day.

Thanks,

Dave

Hi Eileen,

The first time I heard about the existence of *The Exorcist*, I was only about fourteen years old and much too young to see it in theaters. At the time, I was used to Dario Argento's movies and thought *Profondo Rosso* was as scary as you could get, but then a friend of mine told me about some "record-breaking" horror movie about a possessed girl spitting something green. I was fascinated by this, but terrified at the same time. In 1989, the movie was released for Italian television. I was beside myself with joy but worried at the same time! The advertisement was on the national networks even two or three times per day. I couldn't wait to see it. In the meantime, I was wondering if this movie would scare me too much that I would not be able to sleep peacefully anymore. I desperately wanted to see it but I was really worried. After seeing *The Exorcist*, my perception of horror changed and no other movie will ever be equal to it, even after forty years! I can't stop making comparisons with it! Also, the soundtrack contributed to making the whole thing more disturbing, grotesque and terrifying. For me, it still remains one of the best masterpieces of horror!

Sylvia

When I was younger, my dad played *The Exorcist* on Halloween. He had all the lights out. He showed me the devil face while it was on pause and it stared at me. I was scared shitless and to this day, I am still scared to look at that face. I can't close my eyes at times without seeing that white, pale face with jagged teeth and red around its eyes and black mantle. That movie is hard for me to watch and it's the only movie that scares the shit out of me.

Ravyn

When I first saw *The Exorcist* at eight years old, it opened my eyes; not only to Horror, but to the power of Cinema. From that point on I became obsessed with film and, twenty-six years later not much has changed. I am now involved in writing and making films. I have traveled the world showing my films at various festivals and I do believe that, without *The Exorcist*, I would not be doing this or have seen the places I have seen or met the people I have met. *The Exorcist*, for me, shows the very power of film and of the mavericks who dared to make something that would defy convention. It shows us all that if you live without fear of opinion and have an idea, you are the only person who can stop yourself.
Anonymous

When I was about thirteen years old, I saw *The Exorcist* for the first time on French TV with my Dad. I was so scared we had to switch off the TV for like twenty minutes, then we started to watch the movie again and I didn't sleep all night. Then fast forwards to 1994: I'm a Film and Drama student at the University of Reading, in the UK and *The Exorcist* is playing on a Saturday Night at midnight. And I'm told that *The Exorcist* and *A Clockwork Orange* are still "BANNED" in the UK and can ONLY be shown at midnight on a Saturday. Go figure. Anyway, me and my classmate Kelly Smith, who also became a Horror director, go see the movie, which I had seen a bunch of times on TV and video tapes...Seeing it on the big screen was quite a different experience. It was so intense, there's a moment--when Regan screams while the scanners spin around her head--when I almost fainted on a guy sitting next to me. As a horror fanatic, I had already seen most scary movies by then and never had I felt physically sick from watching a movie. When Kelly and I went back to our student houses, I was so scared I asked Kelly to stay with me until the sun came up as there was no way I was going to get any sleep in the dark. Kelly and I were talking about that the other day on Skype while trying to come up with a new concept for a horror movie. We've both become horror directors after our time at Reading University.

Julien Magnet, Director of *Face in the Crowd*

The Exorcist is still by far, with no contest, the scariest movie I have ever seen. It has stuck with me over the last thirty years and is hands down the only horror film I cannot bring myself to watch alone. It has affected my career as a horror filmmaker and my senses as a film lover. Nothing has come close to my high level of anxiety and fear from films that have come after.

Tammi Sutton

My brother George was 6 years older than me, a real horror lover and a bit of a psychological sadist as well. From the time I was 5 years old he would terrorize me with his homemade monster masks, haunted houses in the basement and scratches on my window in the middle of the night. But nothing he did ever terrorized me more than when he decided to treat me to dinner and movie. That movie was *The Exorcist*. I knew a little bit about the movie mainly that the little girl in the film became increasingly ugly and horrifying as the movie progressed. In the beginning of the film Reagan appears normal. No worries there. Then as the movie goes on she becomes pale, sunken-eyed and sickly. At this point I turned to my brother and asked "Does she get any worse than that?" He smiled and said, "No, that's as bad as it gets. Don't worry." Of course he was very, very wrong. When Reagan was at her very worst, right before she pukes the pea soup on the priest out comes my brother with a VERY rare steak, mashed potatoes and of course, green peas! I nearly vomited right there. And as I slept alone that night, my brother came into my room and lifted the bed up and down off the floor - over and over again while I screamed my poor head off! Up to this day, even though I am a huge horror fan and collector, I refuse to watch *The Exorcist* alone.

Joyce, NY

CHAPTER ELEVEN

After Shooting *The Exorcist*

The Exorcist was completed on December 4, 1973, just in time for the film to be considered for an Oscar in 1973. In order to be eligible for a nomination in a given year, a film must be shown at least once during that calendar year. Even if it's pulled and re-released the following year, it can still be considered for an Oscar in the year it was first released. This happens quite often (i.e. Titanic, Avatar, etc.). So, Friedkin finished the editing in time for a Dec. 26 release.

Between the end of filming and when I moved out to California, I busied myself with several projects. One of which was a commercial in which I got to play a bride. I got a call from my agent and she told me I would be working with Doris Roberts. Of course, Doris had already done a ton of work but she wasn't quite the celebrity she became after *Remington Steele* and, later on, *Everybody Loves Raymond.*

So, off I went with the wardrobe stylist into downtown New York City to the garment district to find a wedding dress. I have to admit, having never been a bride, there was definitely something magical about trying on, "the dress," even if it was only for a commercial.

The wardrobe person had me try on a ton of them. Some were very nice and some were just okay, but then we found the perfect dress. Even in my tiny, tomboyish frame, I had never felt so pretty in my life. I stared at myself in the mirror for quite a while and thought, *so this is how I'm going to look when I get married.* It was a moment I hadn't experienced before, so I decided to stay there and savor it for as long as I could.

The set had been made up to look just like a wedding reception. There were extras dressed in suits, tuxes, gowns and dresses--even the tables were adorned with flowers, candles and color-matching accents. I was introduced to the director who quickly explained how the shoot was going to go, and then I was whisked away to the makeup room. That's where they made me into the beautiful, blushing bride I never truly saw myself to be.

Admittedly, it was another one of those magical moments. I stared at myself in the mirror in awe. It was certainly quite a change from the face I saw in the mirror each day on the set of *The Exorcist.* And yet, ironically, I still didn't even recognize myself. The commercial was an ad for a product called, "Fasteeth," an adhesive that would keep false teeth on. And while I did not have false teeth, the "father" of the bride did.

The spot (in the industry, commercials are referred to as "spots," for anyone who's keeping track of jargon) takes place after the wedding ceremony, just before people are sitting down to eat and Doris and I wondered if "Dad" would have any trouble eating the food with his dentures. Of course, with Fasteeth, he could, and so the spot showed the rest of us dancing and smiling throughout the commercial. This would be the only bridal gown I would ever get to wear.

The other project I took was actually my favorite commercial of all time. I shot an ad for Vernor's Ginger Ale in which I got to play a jockey. When I went to the audition, they asked me why they should believe I could ride a race horse. They were also auditioning real jockeys. I remember saying during the audition, "Do you think I am crazy enough to risk this face just for a commercial?" Apparently it was enough to win them over.

The commercial was shot in Central Park, right across from my apartment on Sixty-Fourth Street. When I got to the set, I eyed two horses. One was big. Like, REALLY big, as big as a Clydesdale, but not actually a Clydesdale. It was also much thinner and very sleek. At my height, I came up to where the two front legs go into the chest and had to peer upward to see the horse's face.

The other was sort of an average-sized race horse. Having had plenty of horse-riding experience growing up, I can safely say I had never ridden a race horse until then. I also wasn't exactly sure what the commercial entailed. For instance: was I going to have to race around the park? Was I going to have to race...gulp...the BIG horse? I started praying to my non-existent God they'd set me up on the smaller horse.

Luckily for me, they did put me on the smaller horse. And I didn't have to ride anywhere. In fact, I didn't even move. All I had to do was dismount from the horse, take off my jockey's hat, pick up a can of Vernor's and drink it. That's all.

Things did get a little dangerous when the horse handler wanted to help me get back on the horse. He gave me a "leg-up," which I didn't need because I could throw myself up onto the horse. However, the added lift from the handler sent me up and over, leaving me upside down, holding onto the horse's neck.

The last "project" I worked on prior to moving out west was marrying my first husband, Richard. Now, most people probably wouldn't consider marriage a "project." In fact, I wouldn't consider it a project either. On the other hand, I consider my marriage to Richard more like a living hell.

The Bane of Eileen's Existence

It was Thanksgiving, 1973, and a friend from Manhattan had invited me to a party. I told my parents I wouldn't be joining them for dinner and my mom was furious.

Even as she laid on one guilt trip after another on me, I remained adamant. Why? I guess I was just young and stubborn and my friend was more important than my family that day. And I suppose I wanted to brag about working on *The Exorcist*. Oh, how I lived to rue that choice.

When I arrived at my friend's apartment, I immediately asked for some "liquid nerve-calmer" and went about mingling. It wasn't long before I saw him, the man who would eventually be the cause of most of (if not all) my nightmares.

Isn't it funny how something so seemingly small and minute can completely alter your life? If I had only listened to my parents, went to their house for dinner, life would have been totally different. But, I didn't listen. I'd gone to the party. And I met   *him*.
Richard wasn't handsome in the classic sense. He was about five-foot-six, with blonde hair and bright blue eyes. But I was more than just a little attracted to him that night. I went home with him.

He was a poet and an artist and very much a romantic. He would write me these fabulous poems. He had an idea for a very funny comic strip with bubbles around the characters' heads to show what they were thinking. He'd also just quit his job the same day we met. The jobless, artistic type. Quite the charmer. Somehow, it worked on me. A friend of mine had told me early on to watch out for this guy, he wasn't all that he seemed, but I didn't care. I wanted someone in my corner.

Something else influenced my decision to include Richard in my life. A movie called *Mahogany* had just come out and the tagline was something like, "Success is nothing if you have no one to share it with." Granted, I had my friend Jo, but she was dating someone and had long since moved out. There was also a billboard for the movie, including the same tagline that I saw every day as I walked home to my apartment on West Sixty-Fourth Street where I now lived alone. That advertisement was a constant, staunch reminder of how lonely I was. My twin sister had gotten married and throughout the entire wedding, I had to endure the question, "So Eileen, when is it going to be *your* turn?" It was depressing. I still loved acting and each new project was more exciting than the last, but I had nobody to share my excitement with. I suddenly found myself with nobody to take care of, except me. After all, Marianne now had a husband who could take care of her, so she didn't need me anymore. In the end, I chose Richard. He became my person; the one who would share my success with me.

Did it have to be Thanksgiving night that I met Richard? Of all the 365 days and nights of the year, our relationship had to begin on one of the biggest American holidays. Every year when I watch the Thanksgiving Day Parade, I think about him and how our meeting changed my entire life's path. I remember that morning, years ago. I was in fact watching the parade from the window of my apartment, which was only about a half-block away. I remember it was a very beautiful day, the first Thanksgiving after *The Exorcist* wrapped. Weird how such a lovely, peaceful beginning to a day ended with me arguing with my parents, ignoring their pleas for me to come over for the holiday and spend time with our family and running to a party to meet the man who would ultimately become my ex-husband.

I don't think I ever really loved him. I just loved the idea that he loved *me*. My parents told me if we didn't have a big wedding, they'd give us the money they would have spent on the ceremony. So, we ran away to Miami to get married. The man who married us wore a horrible toupee and we ended up suppressing a lot of laughter throughout the entire ceremony. Unfortunately, it was the only time we laughed in the year we were married.

When we came back to New York, my parents had a reception for us at their house on Long Island. It was a very wet, rainy day. From the time we arrived until the time we left, it poured buckets on us. So much for the belief in wedding-day rain being a sign of good luck. I don't think we managed to squeeze an ounce of luck out of all that water. Our car managed to stall out after we left our apartment.

We were halfway to my parents' house when the engine just quit. Richard, never the handy man, insisted on getting under the hood to try to figure out what was wrong. In the end he couldn't fix the problem so we ended up calling Triple A and they got the car started. But the damage had already been done. Richard was soaked and without a dry change of clothes. He was miserable the whole time. I was miserable too, all the while forcing a thin smile.

As with all receptions, we *did* have a photographer, but the film got damaged and thus, we have no record of that horrible, momentous event. We're probably better off there is no record of that day, I found out later on Richard spent the entire time making passes at friends and other family members. It was embarrassing. What was equally embarrassing, if not more so, is that this behavior was not a one-time thing, or even an occasional thing. It happened *all* the time. I didn't know any of this then. I never found out until the marriage was over.

My First Screening of *The Exorcist*

The day of the New York screening of *The Exorcist*, Richard and I attended together. The screening was held at a theatre on Third Avenue. I remember the entire place was full.

There was a noticeable air of expectation; people going in, bracing themselves for the forthcoming scares, couples holding each other as they walked through the ticket line, hoping they wouldn't be *too* scared. As an actress in the film, I truly didn't know what to expect. I'd simply hoped the audience would enjoy it and that it would be successful. Richard and I found a couple seats toward the front and we settled in, along with the rest of the audience, for what would be an amazing night of filmmaking.

As the movie progressed, I casually looked around at the people near us. I saw men and women glued to the screen by fear and apprehension. Shock and terror on everyone's faces. It was a moment I'll never forget. A moment that amazed me and first made me realize I was a part of something really special.

Then the scares came often. From the bed shaking and rocking under little Regan, to the demon's voice, to the exorcism at the end, the film didn't let up. Even through the "non-scary" moments, the film kept an edge of uneasiness that was palpable throughout the audience. I never even thought about what Linda did vs. what I had done--the transformation from Regan into the Demon was so seamless and complete. I marveled at the on-screen results produced by Dick Smith and Marcel Vercoutere, two geniuses of makeup and effects.

When the movie was over, there was a moment of deathly silence. I briefly had the insecure feeling people didn't like the film. But, insecurity disappeared as thunderous applause erupted throughout the theater. It seemed to go on and on. Meanwhile, I hardly realized I was one of the many who was applauding. It was a fantastic movie from beginning to end and

I couldn't have been happier or more proud to have been even a small part of it. Richard was applauding, too. I felt blessed that someone was there to enjoy the moment with me, even if it was him.

Richard: My Husband, My Agent?

After the screening, life went on for the most part. At some point during our marriage, Richard began to act as my manager. One day, I had just gotten home and he told me Warner Brothers had called. My heart was immediately in my throat. I couldn't believe it. *Me?* Why would Warner Bros. call me? Richard explained they wanted me to come out to Los Angeles to meet with them and Billy Friedkin. To say I was honored would be an understatement. Being invited to come to Hollywood after having worked into what would go on to become the most talked-about film of the year was overwhelming. I called my agents and told them about the invitation. They scheduled meetings for me with three different Hollywood agents. Unlike in New York, where you could have multiple agents booking you for multiple jobs, you could only have one theatrical agent in Hollywood. I suddenly felt like I was really on my way and that my dream was about to come true.

The first sign that something was wrong came after an audition for a shoe commercial. The production company loved me but they felt the client deserved to see a few more choices. They were certain the client would pick me but they asked my agent to send a few more girls for the callback. As life would have it, I did not get the commercial. Another girl who apparently was also about five-foot, two-inches tall with brown hair and a bit tomboyish, got the spot. It was no big deal to me. Hell, by then I'd been doing this long enough to know you win some and you lose some. I was just happy to get a call back.

When I told Richard, he became livid. I'd tried to calm him down, to let him know this is the way things go, that you don't always get the spot and, as an actress, I just have to continue auditioning and when there's an opportunity, my agents would let me know. Richard didn't see it that way.

Without my knowing, Richard called my agents and ripped them apart. "How could you send someone just like Eileen?" he blasted at them. "Why didn't you send a tall blond, instead? You're her agents! Why didn't you protect her?" He was furious. Apparently, he went on and on for a while. My agents didn't take too kindly to his ranting.

If it helps to understand the difference between commercial agents and theatrical agents, I'll explain briefly: Theatrical agents tend not to want too many of the same "kind" of actor, so while a theatrical agent may reject you because they don't want too many "like you." This is precisely how a commercial agent makes his/her money. Commercial agents, unlike theatrical agents, or even managers, handle dozens and dozens of clients. It was their job to send out more girls like me. As an actress, you just have to develop thick skin and understand there are plenty of other girls who look like you. It just comes down to the luck of the draw.

The next time I talked to my agents, they pretty much reprimanded me. They said they didn't appreciate being spoken to like that from someone who wasn't even in the industry. I remember crying on the phone, apologizing repeatedly. They accepted my apology but also warned me to stay away from Richard. They claimed he would ruin my career. I apologized again and said I would talk to Richard. But did I stay away from him? Nope. I didn't listen to my agents. And why would I? I'd made a career out of not listening to people. I didn't listen to the medium on Broadway, the one who saw "demons" all around me. I didn't listen to my parents when they wanted me to come for Thanksgiving. I didn't listen to the girlfriend who'd warned me about Richard and his past. I didn't even listen to my "God nudge" that kept telling me, "Hey, Eileen. Stay in New York. Don't go to Hollywood. It's not your turn yet." Hell, even our dog, Kismet, hated Richard. She was a husky, which is a pack dog, and they typically want company all the time. So when she was home alone, she would chew up everything. Well, *almost* everything. She chewed up Richard's suits, his medicine bottles that sat on the end of the table next to the bed, his shoes. Never once, however, did she ever chew up anything of mine. I guess that's why they're called, "animal instincts."

CHAPTER TWELVE

Controversy

The Golden Globes soon came and went. Linda earned a Globe for her work on *The Exorcist*. Simply put, she was *amazing*. Forget about being twelve-years old, she was just great. She stood toe-to-toe with some of the best in the business and never backed down. Friedkin provided guidance, sure, as all directors do, but it was Linda in front of the camera. From the work she did with those medical experiments, to the torture of having to sit for hours on end while Dick Smith, and others, applied layers and layers of makeup, to having to utter those horrific expletives take after take. I thought she was brilliant. And she took it all like a pro. I applauded (literally) when they announced her name during the awards show. I was genuinely happy for her. I still had no idea about what was coming to me as I was headed to California.

We arrived in Hollywood with Kismet in tow. Hollywood looked just like I'd seen in the movies and on television. The sun even seemed to shine brighter there. The sky was much bluer than I'd remembered back in New York.

After all, there wasn't any smog in those days, at least not like there was on the east coast.

Palm trees lined the streets. The buildings sparkled, reflecting the sun's rays. It all looked so magical. And movie stars! I was finally where the movie stars are. I had to pinch myself to make sure I wasn't dreaming. It felt like all my wishes were about to come true. Every single negative thought I'd had until then was gone.

We settled in at a hotel called, The Sunset Marquis, for a couple days until we found a more permanent place to stay. To my delight, Howard Fast (of *Spartacus* fame) was staying there as well. Fast was a hero of my liberal mother. And *Spartacus* was very instrumental in helping to end the boycott of Directors, Writers and Actors who had been investigated by the House Committee on Un-American Activities. At the time, those who were under investigation were unable to work for years. But, instead of taking it on the chin, many of these fine people worked under false names in order continue their careers.

All this foolishness started to come to an end when Stanley Kubrick and Dalton Trumbo came along and produced and directed *Spartacus* starring the legendary Kirk Douglas and Tony Curtis. When Howard was allowed to use his real name, it was a victory for those who'd been "blacklisted." Shortly after, more people were able to continue using their real names. I remember watching TV in our room at The Sunset Marquis. I reached out and touched the TV screen and allowed a new realization to sink in: there was a very strong possibility that being cast in a show might actually be more than just a dream now.

Hollywood, unlike New York, is a very large film community. New York is much smaller and for the most part, most people know what everybody else is doing. In other words, news travels fast in New York. And although I agreed not to talk about the film or my part in it, everybody knew I was shooting *The Exorcist*. From my agents to their clients to my agents' colleagues and their colleagues' clients--most people just knew. It wasn't a big secret. Casting notices had gone out so everyone knew they were casting someone to play this demon in the movie, mainly because Linda was deemed too young to perform certain scenes. I would walk into an office and the producer or casting director would ask how the shoot was going. It was common knowledge. Not being familiar with the Hollywood community, I had assumed it was the same with folks on the west coast as well. Unfortunately, this was not the case.

While I was taking acting classes under Warren Robertson in New York, I was friends with a young actress (whose name I'll never remember) who was also friends with a woman who wrote for the *Los Angeles Times* in California. She

204

had told her journalist friend about me and how I was moving out to Los Angeles at the invitation of Warner Brothers. Before I knew it, a story was released about an actress from New York who had claimed to have done all the possession scenes from the film. The same scenes for which Linda Blair had just won the Golden Globe.

I started freaking out. Soon, the story was in all the gossip columns. Joyce Haber, who was enormously popular, and the Hedda Hopper of her day, had taken the story and ran with it as far as she could. I remember Richard and I were having dinner with TV producer, Leslie Stevens (of *Gunsmoke* fame) and he said something I'll never forget: "No worries, Eileen. You have nothing to worry about as long as they spell you're name right."

But that wasn't true at all. My "secret" was in *The Los Angeles Times* and I still had said nothing. I hadn't gotten a phone call from anyone at the studio yet, but I knew it was coming. They were going to hate me, if they didn't already. I just wanted to turn and run, run all the way back home to New York where there were still people who knew me and believed me.

But I didn't. I guess I just hoped it wasn't as bad as it seemed and, eventually, everything would work out for me. After all, I still had meetings with three different agents and a meeting at Warner Brothers with Billy Friedkin. I would just calmly explain what had happened, that I'd kept my word and would always keep my word.

"You'll Never Work in This Town Again!"

The call finally came from someone at Warner Brothers and we arranged a meeting for the next day. I was so excited. Not only would we discuss this awful miscommunication that had ensued and they would finally understand I had kept my word, I was going to arrive on a movie studio set for the very first time. Warner Brothers, of all studios, is the first home of so many stars. And so I nervously got dressed. What should I wear? Something that screamed of a teen-aged Regan? Something much more sophisticated and "movie-starrish?" I stopped fussing over my clothes long enough to find something conservative.

Driving in Los Angeles really frightened me, for a while. Unlike New York, where people stopped to let you on the highway, it seemed drivers of the Los Angeles Freeways would just go. Also in New York, there was so much traffic you rarely got out of first gear. In L.A., it seemed people were always in such a hurry to get to the next light or the next traffic jam. At any rate, I was not yet comfortable with driving as I pulled up to the Warner Brothers studio lot.

I stopped at one of the gates as I'd been instructed and a guard found my name on the list. I wasn't even inside the building yet and my heart was already pounding like it was going to jump out of my body. The security guard gave me instructions as to where I had to go. He gave me a parking pass and I proceeded. I drove through the lot knowing these were the very streets Judy Garland, James Garner, Bette Davis and James Cagney had walked to get to their dressing rooms or the commissary. My eyes must have been as big as saucers. I was so excited I had trouble breathing. I rolled my window down and let the Los Angeles roll through my hair. It was a beautiful day. The sky was true blue and in the distance I could see snow-covered peaks glimmering in the sun. People bustled to and fro, going to shoots or offices or auditions, I assumed. I was now one of them. I felt like I belonged to Hollywood and Hollywood belonged to me. My life was pure joy. I was here! I had made it! The dream was coming true at this moment and in this space.

And then I was there at the office. It was rather nondescript, just a brick wall with a door. Not even a reception area. I took a deep breath, smiled, and walked into the room.

To this day I don't recall who else was in the room with me and Bill Friedkin. I must have had a severe case of tunnel vision because all I saw was the carpet, some chairs, and him-- his venomous eyes were glaring at me. He was pissed. And for good reason. But he was pissed at ME for telling the world Linda had not performed all the possession scenes herself. The reason he wanted the movie-going world to believe a little twelve-year old girl went through this torture herself is because he thought it would make the movie much scarier. So when word got around that Linda hadn't done it all by herself, he was livid. The words, "It wasn't my fault, it wasn't my fault!" screamed in my head, but not out my lips. It was then I knew that no amount of explanation was going to convince him otherwise.

I don't remember everything he said, but I do remember those infamous words: "You will never work in this town again!"

My entire world was crumbling around me. My whole career flashed in front of me. And for a while, I thought I was done. Check that--I *knew* I was done. I mean, come on. When you're sitting in a room in one of the largest film studios in the world and an Academy Award-winning director is screaming at you, telling you you're finished, you can be sure things aren't going to be very good for you.

I tried to explain what happened. I stumbled over my words, tried to make sense of it all, hoping Billy would understand. But he didn't want to listen. He just yelled and yelled. I was too stunned to even cry. In fact, I don't think I cried for a long time. As I sat there in that chair, all I could think was, *This is it. My career is over. My life is finished. My parents were right, I wasn't "good." I would never be "good." I was bad. Jay*

Lowen was right. I will never amount to anything.

I was numb. The only thing I felt was my heart punching the inside of my ribs; but now it was out of fear and dismay instead of excitement. I started to doubt myself. I hadn't done anything wrong. Had I? I had only come to Los Angeles at the behest of Warner Brothers. Why didn't I listen to my God nudge? Why am I here?

Billy left the room and I sat in silence for a while, wondering what would eventually become of me once I left the studio. What would I tell my agents? Where would I go? Would I stay in California? Go back to New York? An office worker came into the room and asked me if I would like a glass of water. I never even spoke. I just shook my head, stood up on shaky legs and walked out of the office.

Walking out of the studio felt like the tornado scene in the *Wizard of Oz*. Except, instead of houses flying around, it was Friedkin's words swirling around in my head, replaying over and over, just as loudly as when I was in that room. And instead of the Wicked Witch of the West, I just kept seeing Friedkin's face staring at me with the most resentful eyes I'd ever known. It's a cruel sort of irony how *The Wizard of Oz*, one of my favorite films ever, was shot on the Warner Brothers lot. As a child, I'd always wanted to go to Oz, except I would have never clicked my ruby slippers and gone back to Kansas. Oh no, I would have stayed in Oz where there was color and magic and

I, Dorothy, was the star and the hero.

I'm not sure what Richard and I talked about when I got back to our hotel. I'm sure we talked about the meeting but, to this day, I don't remember what was said between the two of us. The only thing I do remember from that day is arriving at the beautiful Warner Brothers studio, being in awe of the amazing bungalows and sound stages, and then finally realizing I was the most hated actress in Hollywood.

Did Friedkin really mean it? I'd be able to work again, right? Could I really be blackballed? Did Friedkin have that much power?

I could barely look at Richard. Half of me was scared for my life as an actress. The other half, pissed off. Both Richard and I knew he was the one who'd convinced me to come to Hollywood. He was the one who'd made me believe that Bill Friedkin and Warner Brothers would welcome me with open arms. How did I fall for Richard's bullshit? Chalk it up to being naïve, I suppose. I was even naïve to think nobody would know what Friedkin had said to me. I still had those meetings scheduled with the three agents that my New York agent had set up for me. They wouldn't know about what Friedkin said to me. Would they?

The next day, I called all three of the agents. Not one of them would talk to me. They wouldn't even take my calls. Each time I tried, I spoke with a receptionist who told me they were either no longer interested or had changed their minds. It felt like a conspiracy. Like a losing battle in a war between me and all of Hollywood. The worst part was, I wasn't fighting it. I'd never meant for any of this to happen. Friedkin had accused me of giving the story directly to Joyce Haber, which couldn't have been any farther from the truth. When I look back on it, I can see how it must have looked to them. I'm not sure if I would have believed me either. But I knew what was right. None of it had been done deliberately, not on my part. It was simply a misunderstanding. A *BIG* misunderstanding. And one from which I wasn't sure I'd ever get any kind of redemption.

The same day I tried to call the agents, the story hit the trades. According to the press, I was an extra who had done no acting in New York and was simply trying to attach myself to this star film, *The Exorcist.* An "extra." It hurt so much when I read about it, story after story. I curled up and collapsed on our hotel room floor. I felt so sick. I felt like I could vomit, but my insides were so twisted and clenched, all I could do was cry.

Days went by and I didn't leave the hotel room other than to buy food, which I didn't even want to eat. I tried not to read any more of the stories, but it was impossible. Again, I thought about going back to New York. To this day, when I lie awake at night and can't sleep, I wish I had gone back home. Perhaps with my tail between my legs, to explain to people why it didn't work out. Memories of going back to New York after the Michigan incident haunted me. People still knew me in New York and I could probably get some work. I could just fly back and put all of this behind me.

But that wasn't my dream. My dream was here, in Hollywood. Sure, New York is wonderful and the acting community is a close-knit one, but my dream had always been to become a Hollywood actress. That's when I decided to try and prove I did nothing wrong. Or at the very least, try and set everything right.

Proving Myself

My first stop was the Screen Actors Guild. I walked down Sunset Boulevard, down the block from the famous Schwab's Drugstore--where so many movie stars had been discovered--and into the white, oddly-shaped building, which is where the Guild was during that time, and stepped in front of the receptionist's desk.

"I am here to talk about my work in *The Exorcist*," I said. I could hear the tremble in my voice and I knew the receptionist heard it too. I even felt my face get hot as my nerves began to fire.

"Really?" she said.

I took a deep breath and tried to stay as composed as possible. "Yes. I think I am being treated wrongly and I don't know what to do. I don't want anything. I just want to be able to put this work on my resume."

I was taken into a room to talk to some people--someone who represented the Guild, as well as a SAG lawyer. I told them my whole story from beginning to end. I told them I'd promised not to say anything about my involvement in the film and that I had in fact kept my word. Again, I repeated, "I don't want anything. I just want to be able to put this on my resume."

After the meeting with SAG, I started to feel a little more confident. They seemed to understand and so I took that as a good sign and walked out with my head held a little higher than when I'd come in. As I was walking up Sunset, I stopped in at Schwab's for an ice cream. Secretly, I thought if I stayed there long enough, some filmmaker might come in and discover me. All I could think was, *Lana Turner was discovered here. I could be discovered here!* Then I looked down at my skinny body, at my black, unflattering turtleneck (sans boobs) and a pair of jeans that had seen multiple wears the same week. It was the Seventies--hippies, beatnicks and lots of black eye makeup. I started to think, *Who the hell am I kidding? I'm not going to be discovered at a drugstore.* So I left and drove back to the Sunset Marquis only to find that Kismet had chewed through the carpet of the hotel room.

It was time to leave the hotel and find a permanent place to stay. I also realized I had to give Kismet away. She hated Richard so much and was still chewing his stuff. I found a nice family with a home, a big backyard, and a pool. They were so happy to take her in. Again, it wasn't until later I realized I'd made a huge mistake. I should have given Richard away instead.

And the Oscar Goes to...

Shortly after Richard made a brief stop back in New York to get our stuff, we officially said goodbye to the apartment on West Sixty-Fourth Street and moved into a place on Larrabee Street, not far from the Sunset Marquis. In an effort to keep one foot in New York, we decided to sublet the apartment to Betty Buckley's ex-husband. In hindsight, we should have kept the apartment because somewhere along the way, the ex-husband stopped paying the rent and we lost the place. It was a shame because, at the time, the rent was only $125.00 dollars a month. I could have just paid the rent every month myself and rented it out to folks visiting New York. Oh well. Lesson learned: Don't rent apartments to non-paying ex-husbands of talented Broadway stars.

Back out in California, with the Academy Awards fast-approaching, the story was still making headlines. Being this was all during the same time as the Watergate scandal, some reporters started getting clever, writing headlines like, "THE

GREAT GREEN PEA SOUP WAR!" and "WHO DID WHAT, WHEN!" It seemed like every day the trades were carrying the story on the front page. As a little girl, I'd always dreamed of being written about and talked about on the front pages of the trades--the newspapers that only covered Hollywood news--but this was nothing like I'd ever imagined. They were making fun of me. They were taking shots at me every day and I couldn't even defend myself. Then I started getting the phone calls.

The William Morris Agency came calling by way of a letter. They were perhaps the biggest theatrical agency in the world during that time, handling just about every big name in the industry, including Linda Blair. The letter warned me to "cease and desist" any attempt to put the film on my resume. I received calls from TV shows, network shows. Even Joyce Haber herself called but, by then she had already broken the story in the trades, so I really wanted nothing to do with her.

On the other hand, I thought maybe it would be good to take an interview with the person who was taking the biggest shots at me. I could talk about how I thought Linda had done an amazing job (which is how I truly felt and still feel), how she delivered a very moving, memorable performance in the film and how she'd done the majority of the acting in the film. I could tell Joyce I only did what they asked me to do, which was to play the part of the demon that inhabited Linda's body for only a few specific scenes that required a stronger, more grown-up body. Linda certainly carried the film on her back and I've always been awed by her performance. Ultimately, I thought that talking about this could also make things much, much worse, and I demurred. I just wanted to close my eyes and hide and pretend none of this was happening.

I had no forum to explain my position to put *The Exorcist* on my resume. I wanted to applaud Linda for her work and on her Golden Globe. I wanted to shout from the rooftops that I wasn't trying to take anything away from her. But I had no outlet through which to do so. The trades said there was a lawsuit between me and Warner Brothers, which was, and is, an absolute fabrication. I never tried to sue Warners. The thought never even crossed my mind. For one, who the hell was I to bring a lawsuit against a major movie studio? Who does that? Well, I know Mercedes McCambridge did, and she won. She had been promised a screen credit in the film; however, after seeing her name was absent from the initial release, Friedkin explained there wasn't enough time to add her name to the credits. When the Screen Actors Guild got involved, Friedkin added her credit in the movie where it belonged. Mercedes had won an Oscar for *All the King's Men* and had the clout and money, I assume. But personally, I was just happy I had *any* part in the film. I knew my place. I was just a kid who, thankfully, had been able to support herself as an actress, living in New

York, by appearing in a couple independent films, a couple soaps, a PBS special and a couple renowned off-Broadway plays. Far more than a lot of people, but I was no Mercedes McCambridge.

It got so bad at one point that, at a party I had once attended, an actress I had been talking to said, "Oh no, you can't be Eileen Dietz. Eileen is this blond, 'nowhere actress'" who would do anything to get her name in the paper, including stepping on a little twelve-year old child." I truly felt I was on trial for something and I simply couldn't prove my innocence. I wondered how a defendant in a murder case felt when he/she couldn't find anyone to believe they were innocent. Of course, I wasn't going to jail, but I had no idea where I was going from here.

The Oscars were looming and *The Exorcist* earned nine nominations including: Best Picture, Best Director, and Best Actresses for Ellen and Linda. Meanwhile, the campaign against me and Mercedes continued in earnest. There was a story on the front page of the *New York Times* that suggested Mercedes had been drinking again in order to do the voice of the demon, when in fact she had been sober for years. Little blurbs about me continued to appear here and there as well.

It wasn't until after the Oscars when I found out the film made an extra quarter of a million dollars in free publicity. All people talked about and all they wanted to see was, "Who did what?" A quarter of a million dollars. In 1974, that was damn good money. Sometimes I think maybe that was why they had invited me to California in the first place, to get people talking. But then *The Exorcist* didn't really need more publicity did it?

In the end, *Paper Moon* won Best Picture and Tatum O'Neal walked away with the Oscar for Best Supporting Actress. *The Exorcist* won two awards: Best Screenplay for William Blatty's script and one more to Chris Newman for Sound Mixing. I'm not sure why the film didn't win any more. Some believe the Academy was too scared by the film, or the Academy members just didn't like horror films and didn't believe a horror film should win an Oscar. No horror film before then, had ever won Best Picture before nor best actress, director etc. Perhaps the people who make up the voting membership were not of the millions of people who saw and loved the movie. Maybe it was due to the cover-up; that Billy had actually used six actresses to play Regan and Hollywood didn't like being fooled. Yes, six. There was Linda, me and Mercedes. There was also a lighting double, a stunt double and finally, the girl who did the spider-walk. Oh my, what a genius Billy was, taking the six of us and seamlessly creating a single character! Nobody outside the industry had any inkling there was more than one person involved. Even before I arrived in Los Angeles just about everybody knew that Linda was too young to perform the masturbation scene. I had been hired specifically to do that one scene. But, months later I was still on the set, sitting in the makeup chair and filling in when they called on me.

Perhaps if the filmmakers had said, "Oh yes, we used six people to complete the role of the little girl and demon," then maybe *The Exorcist* would have won the Oscar. I'm sure the movie would have made just as much money, if not more. But I have finally come to believe that a few newspaper articles were not enough to cost Linda the Oscar. Nobody ever said, "Eileen Dietz did ninety-five percent of the work on the film."

For a long time I believed I might have cost the movie their Oscars, but I have come to realize that Mercedes and I really didn't have that kind of power. Could you imagine some indie actress from Queens bringing down a studio film--the scariest movie of all time? God knows it didn't hurt Jennifer Beals in *Flashdance*, or even now when a young ballerina said she shot ninety percent of the dancing in *Black Swan*--a film for which Natalie Portman won the Oscar, anyway.

Horror films simply did not win Oscars up to and including in 1973. The Oscars are voted on by the entire Academy, unlike the nominations and the Golden Globes which are voted on by seventy-five foreign film critics. I just don't think enough Academy members saw the film. The Academy has always been made of up of rather conservative and somewhat older members, and these people simply did not go to horror films.

The *Exorcist* would become known as the scariest movie of all time and would be voted on many top 100 lists--including AFI, as the scariest movie ever. The Oscars have never been a popularity contest for a film and as we know great films are often left out as well as great actors.

Sometimes I wonder if someone told Linda, "Eileen Dietz cost you the Oscar. You didn't win because of her." I can only imagine how heartbreaking that must have been, especially at twelve-years old! For years, I've tried to explain to Linda I never meant to hurt her, to apologize if I had even the littlest impact on what happened. I can understand how she feels, though. After all, who are you going to believe? People who've surrounded you and supported you your entire life, or some actress who spent five months sitting next to you in a makeup chair?

So, the Oscars were over, the fervor eventually subsided and Linda went on to prepare for *The Heretic*. Meanwhile, here I was in Hollywood, still hoping to be a working actress despite all the negative press I had received. Well fortune, again, came calling. I found out Twentieth Century Fox was shooting a television version of *Planet of the Apes* and I thought, *Makeup and special Effects? I can do that*.

CHAPTER THIRTEEN

A Chimp Named Jillian

While Richard and I were still living in the apartment complex in West Hollywood, a woman from the complex told me that Twentieth Century Fox was doing a television version of *Planet of the Apes*. She knew I'd played the Demon in *The Exorcist* and that I'd spent long hours sitting in makeup chairs, so she figured I'd be a shoe-in for something like *Apes*. I had to agree. And, after having portrayed a demonically-possessed little girl, being made up to look like an ape seemed to me to be something I could easily do.

To say I was naïve is an understatement. Then again, naiveté was ultimately what brought me out to Hollywood in the first place. So, I went out to conquer Hollywood, with or without the blessings of Mr. Billy Friedkin.

I drove out to the Fox lot in Hollywood. These days, nobody is allowed on a studio lot without a studio pass. That has to come from the production office of a television show or film and it has to be totally cleared by the same office. Thankfully in the 1970s it was not as it is now (post-2001) where, not only do you have to have your name on a list, but you have to show your driver's license and be completely certified before you can walk on any lot for an audition. So, when I drove up to the Fox studio lot, I pulled up to the gate where Security met me. I told them, "I have an appointment with the Casting Director of *Planet of the Apes*." They looked at me, said, "Okay," and directed me to the casting director's office.

The Fox studio lot was basically an assortment of bungalows and big cavernous studios. As I drove toward the casting director's bungalow, again it was hard not to get swept up by the spirits of great actors and actresses that had come through Twentieth Century Fox over the years. I was both thrilled and humbled as I drove through the lot on my way to meet with the casting director for a major network television show.

I arrived at the office indicated to me by security and walked inside. "Can I talk to Marvin Paige?" I asked the receptionist. I tried to act confident, like I'd been here before, all the while fighting the earthquake of nerves that trembled through my body. She asked if I had an appointment. I answered, "No, but I think he would like to meet me. I just shot a major film in New York." How's that for brass? Luckily for me, it was just enough. She asked me to wait a minute and walked into Paige's office.

From there it was kind of a blur. She must have come out and said to go in because suddenly I was standing in his office. Marvin Paige was sitting at his desk. Luckily for me, he didn't seem annoyed that I'd somehow made it onto the lot *and* into his office without an appointment. He shook my hand and I remember he had a very honest smile. He was pleasant and seemed genuinely interested to meet with me. He asked me what film I had shot so I told him about *The Exorcist*. How I was used to spend upwards of three-and-a-half hours in makeup sessions. I told him I had a ton of patience and, besides my makeup expertise, I was a hell of a good actress. Somehow it worked because he pulled out three pages of a script, which he referred to as "sides," and told me to look at them because he'd like me to read for him.

By now I wasn't as nervous as I'd been before. I was on familiar ground having done my fair share of readings in the past. I knew I could do what he asked and I had a feeling he was confident in my ability to sit still for the ape makeup sessions, which would also be about three hours on average. So I read for the part of "Jillian," a little chimpanzee who falls in love with Roddy McDowell's "Galen" when he stops off at our farmhouse after suffering a broken leg.

When I finished, Marvin looked at me silently for a few moments. I stood there and waited for him to respond--hoping he'd liked what I'd done. Finally, he broke the silence by telling me it was great and that he'd be in touch. I shook his hand and practically floated out of his office back to my car.

Later that afternoon, while I was relaxing at our apartment, Marvin called. He asked me if I would like to play Jillian. It would only be for one episode but it was still a job, a role. In my head, I screamed, *Of course, of course!* Over the phone, I confidently said I would be happy to play her. He told me they were only paying scale--"scale" being the least amount of money an actor can be paid, according to the union--and I told him this was just fine. We ended our phone call after he told me he'd be getting back to me soon with a call time--that's the time the studio wants you to be on the set.

Normally, call time is one hour before set time so you can go into the makeup room and have your hair and makeup done and then be ready to appear on set to block your scenes. Since I needed to be fitted with my chimp makeup, my call time was actually three hours before set time, sometimes more. To me, that just meant I got to be on set longer than most actors, which gave me more time to take in the entire experience-- perhaps a bit more deeply and more appreciatively than others. As I said once already, many actors despise being in the makeup chair for too long, I actually look forward to it.

As I waited for Marvin's call, I suddenly felt like that same young girl, riding the bus home from Michigan, grasping my Equity card, looking forward to what I was certain would be

224

a bright and successful future. Marvin Paige had single-handedly repaired my fractured confidence. Bill Friedkin and the controversy surrounding *The Exorcist* were becoming a distant memory, at least for the moment, because I was back. I was an actress again.

Marvin's call eventually did come and he said they needed me at the studio. Oh, to be wanted again! As an actress, the feeling of being needed is almost better than having the job itself. Getting that phone call, hearing those words; you're *wanted.* You're *desired.* It's almost as if you're perfect.

I then made an appointment to go to the makeup studios where they measured my face so the pieces to make the ape mask would fit. Not quite a life mask, but still a critical part of the process, nonetheless. The extras wore a one-piece mask that didn't have any moving parts. We, who were playing the leads, had makeup that allowed the mouth to move as well as the eyes.

My call time was six a.m., three hours before set time. I hung up the phone and immediately started to dance like Snoopy from the *Peanuts* comic strip. At some point during my euphoric celebration, I realized I had no idea where I was going. I couldn't exactly check out Google maps or MapQuest (as these were to happen far into the future), so I called the studio back and asked for directions.

As I drove out to the set, having absolutely no idea where in Los Angeles I was going other than into a canyon up in the hills, I watched the sunrise from my car. It was a beautiful sight and a wonderful reminder of new opportunities that awaited me.

I walked into the makeup room where there were already about fifteen makeup specialists. A few had already begun working on some of the actors. Others were getting prepared, waiting for more actors to show up. I put my things down and was quickly shown to a chair.

The lead actors (Lonny Chapman, and others) were made up piece by piece with ape prosthetics on the skin and separate jaw pieces, raised eye pieces, etc. It was another lengthy process but the makeup artists, along with being incredibly talented, were also very relaxed and easy-going. I sensed a camaraderie among them and I quickly realized how fortunate I was to be part of such a special team of individuals. Everybody laughed and joked the whole morning as they engrossed themselves in applying makeup and other special effects.

Before I knew it, the three hours had flown by and I was brought down to wardrobe where they gave me an ape suit--a blue smock and a pair of ape feet. Inside the hairy feet was a pair of tennis shoes. Surprisingly, with all the makeup, latex, fake hair and prosthetics attached to my body, in the hundred-degree heat, my feet were the only things to sweat. By the end

226

of a shoot it would feel like I was sloshing around in puddles, but the rest of the costume was entirely breathable and rather fun to wear.

Planet of the Apes

Whenever I'm asked about the things I enjoyed most when I did *Planet of the Apes*, I always talk about the makeup sessions and the time I spent working with Roddy McDowell. He's easily one of the most fabulous people I've ever had the privilege of working with. All the actors on the show were wonderful. They were all gracious and very welcoming, but Roddy really went out of his way to make sure I felt

227

comfortable. And despite the heat, it was some of the most fun I've ever had shooting a TV show. I encourage anyone who can to buy the set of the episodes from the TV show. They're so much fun and similar to all the films, but still remain unique in many ways.

One of the challenges of working as an ape was figuring out how to eat while at work. Most days I was there from sunrise until sunset. And since we couldn't take off our faces, because it would require another three-hour marathon to re-apply, we had to get creative. We couldn't see past the huge jaws protruding outward on the ape face, so we used straws any time we needed something to drink. Then, when we ate something solid, we sat at tables with small mirrors propped up in front of us so we could see where our mouths were.

When the day was over, we'd wrap and everybody would go their separate ways. In the beginning, I would stick around and wait to see where everyone was going for an after-work drink or something to eat. On the set of *Apes*, we were definitely a close-knit group, but when it came to quitting time, everybody had to get home. For some, "home" was Hollywood. For others, it was the Valley or Santa Monica or Malibu, which was about an hour and forty-five minutes from where we were shooting. It wasn't like being in New York where bars and eateries were a stone's throw away from anywhere you stood. It simply wasn't feasible for all of us to go out.

Of course, just as the makeup folks had to remove the "demon" makeup at the end of each day shooting *The Exorcist*, so did the *Apes* crew. This was another lengthy process because the stuff had been on my skin all day, and they had to go slow so as not to hurt my skin. However, leave it to me to defeat the purpose of the careful and practiced routine of makeup removal. I was so excited and happy to be working again that, once, I'd forgotten to wash any of the residual latex and protective gels from my face before I drove home. That night, as I drove off in my car, cherishing the time I'd spent that first day with all those amazing actors and crew members, as well as the time I would spend with them over the next several days, the dust and dirt from the canyon air stuck to my skin and stung my face like lemon juice in an open wound. One would think I'd learned my lesson after the movie-theater-popcorn/salty-fingers-on-the-face incident. But no, such trivial lessons need not be learned when you're living out your dream.

Sala! Sala!

Korg:10,000 B.C., a TV show about Neanderthal families, was another experience that would require a great deal of patience and sitting in a makeup chair for extended periods of time. And yet again, I walked into the production office (because I still didn't know that was something you're *not* supposed to do) and said, "Hey, I just came in from New York

City where I worked on a major film that required long hours of sitting in a makeup chair and I just finished a *Planet of the Apes* episode where I *also* sat for hours being made up to look like a chimpanzee!"

This skill of being able to sit for long hours having makeup and prosthetics applied to my face and body has served me well throughout the years. For *Korg,* I didn't have to read for the part of "Sala," the young cave-girl who runs away from her family to find love. It was a classic Romeo and Juliet story where the families of two Neanderthal kids didn't get along and tried desperately to separate them.

During one point in the episode, my "boyfriend" and I are running through the canyons and he falls, hurts his knee and shouts, "Sala! Sala!" It was an homage to a famous scene in, *A Streetcar Named Desire* when Marlon Brando's Stanley Kowalski falls to his knees, shouting, "Stella! Stella!"

They sent me to a makeup studio where they made a mold for my teeth which sent my already-buck teeth protruded even further from my mouth. It kind of made me laugh at the time because I'd been picked on and called crazy for wanting to become an actress partly due to the fact I was short, had no boobs, and these buck teeth. So, it was kind of ironic that those same buck teeth would play a prominent role during my time on the set of *Korg.* Taking the teeth from the mold they turned my teeth a horrendous yellow/green color. And, much like they did for *Apes*, they had me wear a fake eyebrow piece that made my forehead jut outward about an inch from my face. Hey, we were cave people, after all.

I wanted to go out with the cast after shooting and have some dinner and drinks, but once again, just like the cast and crew on *Apes* did, the cast of *Korg* just got in their cars and went home. I thought, *Oh well*, and went home too.

Looking back now, as much as I wanted to spend time with the casts, I think I equally wanted to spend time *away* from Richard. My marriage was rapidly disintegrating and I didn't want to face up to the fact I was probably better off alone.

CHAPTER FOURTEEN

Marriage Disintegration

After I wrapped *Korg*, I decided it was time to find an agent. I had a meeting with a small "boutique" agency. The agent I met was a very friendly, elderly man. I'm not quite sure how old he was because, as young as I was, everybody seemed old to me. But he had the most sincere smile and I couldn't help but tear up as I told him the whole story about how I left New York to come to Hollywood to further my career. Thankfully, he didn't care about any of it. He didn't care about the studios, either. He also said when it came to small agencies like his, clients typically built up their careers at those small firms until they felt it was time to move on. *Oh no*, I thought to myself. *This man is my savior. He'll be my agent for life.*

After I'd secured an agent, it was time to deal with my relationship with Richard. It had become more than apparent that my marriage was dissolving into nothing more than a shell of a past relationship. As I worked feverishly to secure more roles and more meetings with other studios, Richard wasn't working. In fact, he hadn't worked the whole time we were married. We basically lived off whatever money I was able to pull in from my acting jobs while he sat at home and wrote his comic strip ideas and worked on his paintings, neither of which went anywhere. It probably goes without saying, but there was *no* life in the bedroom. We'd turned into roommates who slept in the same bed and even that was occasional at best. I began to resent him for what he had done, how he conned me into coming to Los Angeles.

We didn't enjoy each other anymore. We didn't go out together anymore. I completely detested the way Richard tried to control everything, how he "knew" everything.

Fortunately for me, Richard made it very simple for me to break off our union--he left me for another woman; an attorney in Los Angeles. At first I felt stupid, delusional. How could I have not seen this coming? I guess I felt like any wife who's been left by a man for another woman. Granted, we didn't have the best marriage (quite possibly the *worst* marriage), but it was familiar. He was someone to come home to, even if I despised him. But now that it was over, what did I have to come home to?

I suppose it could be called "retribution" when, one day, I got a phone call from that attorney. To this day I don't even know why I took her call, but I did. She told me she was having problems with Richard. She asked me, "Was he *always* like this?" I assumed he still wasn't working, was living off of her, attempting to control her life as well. But, she was my ex-husband's girlfriend, so I really didn't give a shit. I stayed on the phone long enough to tell her, "He's your problem now. Enjoy him." And I hung up the phone.

A few years after the divorce, he tried to get my residuals--these are what actors get paid for repeat showings of their films on TV and now, cable. His attempts never amounted to much. He never got a penny from me. He tried though. He wrote me letters all the time, claiming what he was going to do. At first, I was irritated, even a little paranoid. I didn't honestly believe he could touch my residuals, but a part of me just felt like, "What if?" He even called my sister Marianne, once. I was working on *General Hospital* at the time. He'd asked her if he could get in touch with me. She told him to screw off. Eventually, I realized his claims were baseless and I went on with my life, never to hear from him again.

The funny thing about residuals is stunt persons or doubles never earn them. Only actors do (note to those who still label me a "stunt woman" or a "double"). And to this day, I still earn residuals for my work on *The Exorcist*.

Several years ago, I received a message on Facebook. It was from Richard's brother. He informed me Richard had died of a drug and alcohol-induced heart attack. When I read this message, all I could hear in my head was that song from *A Chorus Line* that goes, "...and I felt nothing! NOTHING!"

Nothing. Richard was gone, but that chapter of my life had been closed a long time ago. I was not interested in reopening it.

Movie of the Week

I found out about a movie, called *Helter Skelter*, through my new agent. *Helter Skelter* was to be a movie-of-the-week about the notorious Charles Manson and his gang. Back in New York we were very aware of Manson's gang, and the killings of Roman Polanski's wife. To this day, I sometimes wonder if Roman's life might have changed if his wife hadn't been killed by Charlie's crew of misfits. Perhaps he wouldn't have raped a thirteen-year old girl and fled the country. But I digress...

I'd read about how Manson had been able to recruit many young men and women, kids who were looking for someone, a messiah perhaps, to love them despite their flaws. They were all runaways, running from parents who either didn't love them, want them, or simply didn't understand them. But Manson had found them and made them believe he understood them. He knew what they wanted and he gave it to them. And in turn, those kids did whatever he asked. They even killed for him.

This all sounded a lot like my experience with The Magic Mime Theatre of America. Albeit far more sadistic and violent than director and lead mime, Bob Capri. I remember saying to my friend Jo, back when I was in the Mime troupe, "Man, this feels like some kind of cult." I had no idea at the time I would eventually appear on television as a member of the cult that worshipped Charles Manson. Talk about déjà vu. Strange how life imitates art and vice versa.

Based on my experience with the Mime troupe and partly because I always felt so alienated as a child and teenager, I knew I was a perfect fit for the role. In particular, I found myself drawn to the part of one eighteen year-old girl. A mere child, really, and living on the edge of society who had lost her way. I wrote a letter to the producers, telling them I felt I knew these people, viscerally, and that I understood and felt genuinely sorry for them and the horrendous mess in which they found themselves in. One of the producers read my letter and called me in to meet. He said he was interested in having me for the role of a Manson gang member named Kathy. She was one of the girls who did not go along on the ride that ultimately ended in a massive killing because there was no room in the car for her. So, I was cast as Kathy.

And suddenly, the first of two things that would become a trend throughout my career happened: I didn't have to audition for the project.

While preparing for the role and amid the still-lingering controversy surrounding my involvement with *The Exorcist*, I sought the advice of my good friend, Tom Holland. Tom and I had met back in New York, long before *The Exorcist* and before any of the proverbial "shit" hit the fan. But even after it did, he was never anything but supportive of me (and still is). He understood why I felt betrayed by the filmmakers and he was always there with an encouraging word, making me feel like I belonged in this world, in Hollywood.

Tom always wanted to be an actor but he found his calling in writing, and then, directing. It was doubly rewarding that he eventually made his name in horror films too. First, in *Psycho 3*, and then later on with the original *Child's Play, Fright Night*, and one of my personal favorites, *Thinner*.

Helter Skelter Director, Tom Gries (who sadly died at the young age of fifty-four while playing tennis) had an amazing presence on the set. He wanted everything to look and feel as real as possible. Underneath our dirty, grubby exteriors, we were all nice people and the whole gang became good friends. Outwardly, however, we were all there for Charlie.

Steve Railsback was our Charles Manson. And what a brilliant actor Steve is! Every day, from the moment he arrived on set until the moment he left, he *was* Charles Manson. He even looked like him. Everyone looked like their parts, the girls who in real life ended up serving life sentences for the murders of Abigail Folger and Sharon Tate (Roman Polanski's wife). Steve treated us with all the love and deference that the real Charles Manson had for his gang which included Barbara

Mallory, who looked just like Squeaky Frohm--the girl who eventually pulled a toy gun on President Ford and went to jail herself, Marilyn Burns (who is truly one of the sweetest ladies on the planet and always looks out for others before herself, played Linda Kasabian), and Christina Hart (who played Patricia Krenwinkel) were absolutely amazing in the teleplay. And if you read the news and saw the pictures (i.e. mug shots), you would think they walked right out of Manson's gang. Amazing actresses.

We shot *Helter Skelter* out at what was called Columbia Ranch, which was the same ranch where the gang had lived for a short time during their reign of terror. There was one night-- and this is a tribute to Steve's amazing talent--we were shooting a scene where we all sat around a campfire listening to "Charlie" sing. In real life, Charles Manson fancied himself a songwriter, and in the movie it was no different. The unusual part is, the group was so transfixed on our Charlie that for a moment, it didn't feel like we were shooting a film. It felt real. *Scary* real. Like none of us were actors in that moment, we were all members of Charles Manson's gang. We'd forgotten about the cameras, the lights, the Director, the crew. We were just a bunch of lost souls, listening to our Messiah sing by the fire. Looking back on it, it sometimes feels very bizarre, very surreal how we just lost ourselves in the scene. But then, as an actor, that will happen from time to time. It's one of the things I truly love

238

about this job.

One of the things you need to come to terms with about being an actor is that eventually, you'll have to decide whether or not you're willing to alter your appearance. Then you'll have to decide the lengths at which you'll go to alter it. When I was interviewed for the part of Kathy, they asked me as well as all the "Manson Girls," as we had come to be known, if I would have a problem going bald since the real Manson Girls had shaved heads. Originally I said yes, as did the rest of the girls. However, when it came time to change our appearances, we all decided that going bald might not be in our best interests.

Faced with this united front, the filmmakers decided to use skull caps under which we were able to hide our hair. They also used makeup to produce the swastikas between our eyes. When I saw myself in the skull cap for the first time, and in full makeup, I was terrified. It was weird because when I did *The Exorcist*, I'd been in way more, and far more, disgusting makeup. But the fact that this look represented exactly how the Manson group looked, was unnerving. Half of me felt like I was a real part of the group. It was chilling. And much like I did while shooting *The Exorcist*, I had to tell myself repeatedly, *This is only a movie. This is ONLY a movie.*

I'm not sure why I played so many of these evil kinds of roles in my career. I definitely enjoy the rush of knowing what I'm doing is pretty damn creepy and will move people;

whether to scare them or to make them feel pity or sadness. I don't believe you have to be evil to play evil or to know how it feels to be downtrodden and abused to play a victim, but you do have to have had a taste of it in your life. Something that will come out when subconsciously called upon. And I certainly had plenty of both.

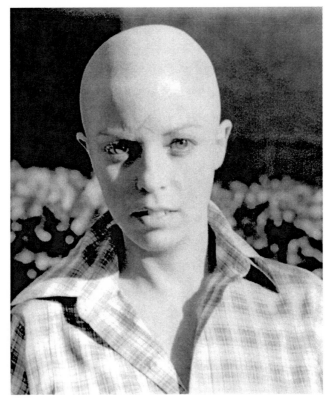

A Manson Girl in *Helter Skelter*

One of the funnier things that happened during filming was during a shoot at a courthouse. We had to shoot during the day at a real working courthouse, and had to shoot around their schedule. So, while court was in session we shot outdoor scenes of us picketing in front of the building. When we were done, the actors were left with their signs, mulling around and waiting for the next scene. At that point, people started coming out of the courthouse; people who really *were* on trial, lawyers, clerks, etc. When they saw us with our picketing signs, they immediately started jeering and screaming at us, telling us to go away. Some of them thought we were the real thing--the real Manson Gang. It took a bit of explaining, but eventually the people coming out understood what was going on. Some of them got a good laugh out of it, some didn't.

One of my favorite parts in the movie comes at the end. It was the last line in the film and, for whatever reason, I was chosen to be the person who delivered it. My character is asked what is going to happen to the prosecutors. I turn to the camera bald-headed, with swastika large and proud across my forehead and I say, "Death! That's what they're all going to get!" It was the first time I'd ever had a final line in any production, and it was a very magical moment in my career. Unfortunately, a decision was made which would lead to the second thing that would become a trend in my career happened; my big scene was removed from the final cut of the film.

The Heretic

News of casting for *The Heretic*, popularly known as *The Exorcist 2*, spread throughout Hollywood. And once again, I wished I had just stayed in New York.

I feel that the producers of *The Exorcist* would have invited me out to Hollywood to play the demon in *The Heretic* if I had just stayed in New York. They probably would have even paid for my trip, put me up in a lovely hotel, and even given me a per diem. I dreamed about how different things could have been if I'd only stayed on the east coast. So once again, I found myself on the proverbial outside looking in. They began shooting the parts of the demon with other actresses. And then, before any of them got on camera, they were let go. All of them. One of them was a girl I knew, and she was heartbroken. I understood how she felt, but I actually took a bit of comfort by this. I'd always thought that anyone could put on some makeup, use a low voice and become the Captain Howdy character. It was rather reassuring to me to find out my talent had gone a bit farther than I'd thought, in helping with the portrayal of the demon. So far, actually, that they eventually *did* call me and asked if they could buy my film from the original and put it in *The Heretic*.

Any actor has the right to refuse the use of previous film in a new film. SAG has very specific rules in place to protect its actors from any wrongdoing in this regard. Any actor and/or his/her agent can negotiate pay for this transference. And if the actor doesn't like the terms, s/he can refuse, simple as that. Then, if a negotiation doesn't happen, and the filmmakers use said film in parts of the new film, they can be fined and the actor will be paid three times his/her original salary for as many days as it took to shoot the sequence.

There was no way I was going to refuse anything. No way was I going to get into any kind of negotiation and they said they would pay me scale for one day. The hurt still ran so deep I didn't want to bring up any more muck. I was afraid, so I simply agreed. Funny. A person could argue I cut a *really* bad deal. That person would be correct. I negotiated myself and I didn't know what I was doing. It would've been a hell of a lot more fun to reprise my role, but that wasn't going to happen, and at least I was in the film. And again, with no credit. All I knew at the time was that I just wanted to put the whole ordeal behind me, which had already become easier said than done.

They have actually used the vomit shot and the Captain Howdy shot in several films and for the promos for *Exorcist: The Beginning*. And, they have always paid me after the fact.

CHAPTER FIFTEEN

Happy(er) Days

It had been a couple years since Richard had moved out and I found myself without a roommate, alone in a strange town. An exciting town, but lonely nonetheless. I was happy to know that Janice Blyth (of the original *The Hills Have Eyes* fame) was also single, living alone, and looking for a roommate. So, I packed up what few possessions I had and moved into a small house with her, in West Hollywood.

Continuing my period of "non-auditioning," I'd met a few people who suggested I do a *Happy Days* episode. The character's name was "Rebecca." She was kind of a misfit, a girl who lived on the edge and didn't fit in. By now you've probably noticed a trend in people recommending me for either roles of misfits who are unloved or characters that required I wear a ton of makeup and no one ever saw my real face. Was I ever insulted by any of this? Not really. It didn't matter what character I was playing, I just loved being on the set of some show, movie, commercial or play. To this day I have never played *Alice in Wonderland*, a kindly mom, or "the girl next door."

I have come to believe that sitcoms are the hardest and scariest things to shoot. It's kind of like a play in that there's a live audience. But you only have days (or sometimes only a few hours) to memorize new lines. On a sitcom the writers often change your lines only moments before you go on. You have to be a real quick study, able to take any direction, and most of all, be supremely confident. As I was.

The shooting schedule for a sitcom is also very intense. A typical sitcom shooting schedule looks like this:

> Tuesday – Actors give a table read of the
> week's episode.
>
> Wednesday – Blocking.
>
> Thursday – Dress rehearsal in front of
> everyone; the writers, producers and
> casting.
>
> Friday – Taping in front of a live audience.

During *Happy Days*, I was back in my element. Rebecca had a 170 or more IQ and no one liked her because she was just too smart. In my episode, Fonzie, Richie, Potsie, Ralphie and I get locked in the back room of Ron Howard's father's hardware store. No one expects to get out until someone comes to the store in the morning. Fonzie and Richie talk about immortality and death while Potsie totally freaks out. It's an amazing episode and the producers of *Happy Days* ran it on Nickelodeon over and over.

The show was always listed in *TV Guide* (this is back when people needed a guide) and it was quite a thrill when I found my name was the only one listed. I was back again and climbing upward! Shooting a sitcom was amazing. The makeup and wardrobe departments did wonderful work changing me into a child of the fifties. My hair was styled into a huge bouffant. I wore a red sweater, a long felt like skirt, bobby socks and saddle shoes. I was able to disappear into another character: Rebecca. You can still find the episode on cable by searching for *Happy Days*: "Time Capsule."

It was all very exciting and the closest I'd come to doing a live stage play since I was in New York. Of course the live applause was very welcomed and something I had not experienced since I'd done live theater. Interestingly, the episode played on my birthday, January Eleventh.

Scuba Diving is Heaven Upside Down

I then, in a roundabout way, landed a role in the TV soap opera, *Guiding Light*. I was auditioning for a completely different soap, *One Life to Live*. They flew me out to New York for the audition and booked a room for me at The Plaza Hotel. I promptly called Jo and asked her to come stay overnight with me. She did, and after a long and heartfelt hug, the first thing we did was order room service. It was just like old times while we ate together in one of the most famous, old hotels in New

York City. We were just like the two girls drinking wine at The Monk's Inn and watching the "rich" people walk by. We took a long walk along Central Park East and watched the horse carriages take their occupants around the park. We watched people walking their dogs. It was so great and so familiar. We hadn't seen each other in several years and spent the whole night before my audition catching up.

The next day after the audition, which I was sure had gone well, I fantasized about getting the soap and moving back to New York, since it was for a multi-year contract. I ended up flying back to Los Angeles a few days before my agent called and told me they felt that I was too young and "unsophisticated-looking" for this particular role. Oh well. I'd been rejected before. As an actor, you get used to losing more than you win. And you must, for your sanity, get to the state of mind that you know how good an actress you are and that you lost the part for reasons outside your control (e.g. you were too short, too tall, not blond, too skinny, too fat or simply the other person up for the role was someone's niece, wife, sister, lover…).

Still, rejection can be a hit to the ego, but in this case it turned out to be a blessing in disguise. The producers at *Guiding Light* asked other casting directors if they knew anyone who could play a kid sister to one of the cast members on their show. The casting director from *One Life to Live* sent them a copy of my audition tape and they cast me without my having to audition a second time. I gladly accepted their offer and I was off to shoot in the Bahamas!

Guiding Light was the first soap opera to ever shoot on location, and for a brief period of time, I got to shoot a TV show in one of the most beautiful parts of the world. What better way to spend a few days working? It did seem a bit strange to me that nobody had ever asked if I could swim. Especially since I would be playing the part of a woman who drowns while scuba diving.

I ended up going down five days early in order to take scuba diving lessons before being thrown into the water (literally and figuratively). I remember the scuba teacher telling me, "If you don't want to take the dive you don't have to." Really? The production company of the show had paid me to go down to the island early. I had the most amazing room in a hotel right on the beach. I had signed a contract to play the role of Lynette Waterman, I had to take the dive, and was glad I did. It's so hard to describe but it was like heaven upside down. There were beautiful fish swimming by, wonderful coral and white sand. It was totally peaceful. I really didn't want to come up. Reality was just as good, if not better, than my acting life: a beautiful hotel on the beach, a per diem to eat as much as we wanted, and a weekly pay check. Once again I had to pinch myself to make sure this was real.

I do remember a lunch they provided during the shoot, which was basically island food that consisted of a lot of beans. Beans while encased in a rubber scuba suit? Not a good idea. But I guess the scuba guides were okay, because they ate away. I wondered if they had a special outlet for gas. Or they simply learned how to not fart.

The crew was also amazing. I will always remember the Cinematographer--he was a slightly older man, a bit roly-poly, and oh so nice. But the poor guy's face was lobster-red and he had scarlet sun-burned marks on his legs where the water stopped.

The *Guiding Light* experience was also where I really learned how to do multiple takes. While filming one particular scene, the director told me, "When you're doing a take, do as few things with your hands as possible because you're going to have to duplicate it over and over." I've carried that valuable lesson with me to every TV show I've ever done.

An amazing man named John Paquin directed the episodes. He was a lot of fun. And when you have all of this, sun, beautiful weather, great crew, plus a director who really understands actors and loves them and loves working with them, life as an actress doesn't get much better. John brought down his wife, actress JoBeth Williams, and we had a lot of fun hanging out together. Even now they are a working couple.

My time on the set of *Guiding Light* was brief. I knew my character was going to die so I enjoyed every moment on the island. My past mistakes and bad choices seemed to wash away into the ocean with the outgoing tide. I was so happy and content in Paradise. We did go back to New York and shot several more episodes, out of sequence (i.e. we shot what happened before Lynette died), and then it was over.

Goodbye, Daddy

When I was finished working on *Guiding Light*, I lived in the City for a short while before moving back to Los Angeles. By that time my dad's health had begun to fail. He and my mother had been working at his studio together for years. They carpooled into the City every morning and, to my delight, they really enjoyed the time they spent together. My mom worked as a bookkeeper in my dad's studio. She had joined Weight Watchers, slimmed down, cut her hair like a pixie and dyed it from gray to a subtle strawberry-blonde. With her new appearance, she felt confident enough to hold her own among the other models.

After my dad's heart attack, he could no longer perform his job at the level needed to run the business so they sold the studio, sold the house in Bayside, and moved to Florida. They held a huge garage sale to help pay for a place in Miami. Sadly, I just couldn't bring myself to go. I especially couldn't bear to see them sell *my* gargoyles. When I was just a child, those statues had represented my primary means of escape, even if it was only a mental one. I never went to see my old house before they sold it.

Unfortunately, and because of my father's poor health, the move to Miami came just a little too late. My dad had always dreamed of a retirement full of relaxation, travel and fishing. Jay had also moved down to Florida, so at least my dad had his good friend with him. They'd meet often for dinner or drinks, but my dad no longer had the strength to do the things he loved. He'd always wanted to buy an RV and travel across the country. But, he was a hard worker, and it was that work-'til-you-die mentality that eventually did him in. Had my mother and father moved to Florida about five or ten years sooner, I'm sure he would have had the retirement he'd always wanted.

My father passed away in 1978, at age sixty-eight. I went to see him just before he died. I remember he looked very skeletal. Even as a grown-up, it was difficult to even look at him directly. He insisted on driving us home from the airport. Everyone in Miami drives about ten miles per hour in these enormous cars. It made me nervous as he drove on the edge of the highway. I eventually convinced him to always let me drive after that. It was also the last time I saw him before he died.

Deni, Marianne and I flew down for the memorial service--he was cremated so there was no funeral. I remember

Deni and me laughing nervously because there was a huge coffin there and we wondered if he was in it or if it was just for show.

My dad never got to see me in *General Hospital*. I would have loved for him to have seen me on that show before he died. I'm pretty sure he would have been proud of me. We never had the greatest relationship especially when I was young, but as I got older I think he probably did the very best he could and was only against me having an acting career because he wanted to protect me. I guess I was just too busy being a rebel to notice.

The Man Who Never Wanted to Marry an Actress…Did

When I got back to Los Angeles, I didn't waste any time looking for my next job. I did an Arthur Miller play, called *After the Fall*, with the Company of Angels Theatre. The play was based on Miller's relationship with Marilyn Monroe. And I suppose we could file this under the category, "Truth is Stranger than Fiction." The actress who played Marilyn was Julie Cobb, daughter of Lee J Cobb. Now, I haven't become close with many people throughout my life, and Julie and I weren't best friends, but I was thrilled to tell her the story about "Whooshee," and the limo ride I shared with her dad. She got a good laugh out of it. I'm sure it was only one of many great stories she'd heard about her father.

I was hanging around the theatre one day when two of the members of the company came to me and said they needed someone to help produce Tennessee Williams' *Cat on a Hot Tin Roof*. It was across town at a place called the Barnsdall Gallery Theatre. I had no previous production experience, but we weren't performing Miller's play at the moment, so technically, I wasn't doing anything else. I enthusiastically agreed to produce it.

The Tech Director and Light Designer at The Gallery Theatre was a man named Thomas Albany. He was kind of hiding when we got there, but I eventually got to meet him. I remember being very taken by his great, deep blue eyes. The first day at the theatre, whenever I passed by him, I got lost in those eyes. As if he was staring right through me, into my heart, watching it beat just a little faster every time I saw him.

One night after a long rehearsal, Thomas asked me if I would give him a ride home to West Hollywood. Some jerk had cut him off the night before and Thomas swerved to miss him, hit a concrete wall, and totaled his car. Luckily, his completely metal-framed Saab protected him enough and he walked away unscathed.

On the way home from the theatre we stopped off at an all-night place to have something to eat. We literally ended up talking all night long. The sun actually came up while we were at the restaurant. It was when we saw the sun, and after a

253

long time spent staring doe-eyed at each other's faces, we decided it was time to go home. We still hadn't run out of things to talk about, but it was a new day and we knew we'd be seeing more of each other. Much more...

I'll never forget the song we heard on the radio as he drove me back to my apartment that first night/morning. Meatloaf's, "Paradise by the Dashboard Light" had been playing. Meatloaf crooned, "...Do you love me? Will you love me forever? Do you need me? Will you never leave me?..." as we drove over the hill.

We never spent a night apart after that (until I started doing horror conventions and went on location for films, but that was much later). I had an apartment in the valley and Thomas had his place in West Hollywood. Thomas called our apartments the "Winter/Summer Palaces" but they were hardly palatial. My place was large but it had a stucco ceiling and no personality except for my collection of antique mirrors that adorned the dining room wall. Thomas lived in a small bungalow on the other side of the hill that made up Laurel Canyon. His place was so small we used to joke that if you sneezed in the bathroom by the bedroom, someone would say "God bless you" from the kitchen.

One day, while paying our bills, we decided it was foolish of us to pay separate rents. So, along with being in love with each other, we moved in together to save money.

Me and Thomas, Young Love

The drive between our two places just wasn't long enough to hear that entire Meatloaf song. Several weeks and many, many years later we're still together. I like to remind him, from time to time, about how when we first met, he had said to me, "I hate actresses. I never want to end up with an actress." I had told him, "Well that's too bad sweetheart, because there's nothing else I've wanted to do with my life since I was seven years old." I guess that's because he worked with actors all the time at the theatre. I guess I either wore him down enough, or he just never hated actresses as much as he thought he did. I tend to believe it was the former.

Ironically, it was just a few years ago that we finally did get to hear the end of Meatloaf's epic song. Funny, we'd heard

255

it played on the radio so many times. It's kind of appropriate, in a way. Thomas is everything I've ever wanted in a man, and then some. And I will certainly love him to the end of time. We simply choose to ignore the end which says, "And so I am waiting for the end of time...so I can end my time with you."

Thomas took this Headshot - His Loveliest "Monster"

Perhaps equally as ironic, Thomas was quite the monster aficionado. Having collected pictures of monsters like, Frankenstein, Dracula, Wolfman, etc., from various monster magazines as a child, he posting them all over his bedroom walls. So not only would he eventually marry an actress (which he claimed he never would), but he'd marry one that had spent the majority of her professional life emulating monsters.

The Clonus Horror

The Clonus Horror was a fun--a sci-fi film way ahead of its time. In the movie, clones are bred to be used as replacement parts for the elite. All these political people like the President and Vice President are cloned. The film takes place in an isolated desert compound called *Clonus,* which is where all the clones are made, including a soon-to-be-president-elect Jeffrey Knight (Peter Graves). I was cast for the part of a young girl--a clone--who tries to convince her boyfriend not to go on a trip to the "factory" where they take the clones and harvest their parts so these political figures can have immortality.

Secretly, I'd hoped to be cast for the lead because I knew the director and the producer. I thought maybe they would notice me and recast me as the lead. Of course, they hadn't envisioned me for the role and, despite all the work I'd done up to that point in my career, I was still too timid to ask to read for the lead part. I still hadn't realized I had created most of my own invisibility by not speaking up. Even Thomas had suggested, "You should read for the lead role." But again, I dismissed the notion. I thought, *once they see me again they will see how perfect I am.*

In the end, they didn't ask me to read. And when the movie was over, they talked about what a fine film it was and how it was destined to become a classic, which it did. But, they'd lamented about how it was "too bad the lead actress was too old and couldn't act." When I told them, "Well, you could have used me," they responded, "We never thought about it. We didn't know you were interested in the lead role. How come you didn't say something?" I never told them as much, but I was still insecure and hadn't said anything before because I couldn't risk them saying "no" to my face.

The movie ended up being quite the cult hit with Sci-Fi aficionados. It even gained a little notoriety a few years ago when the director, Robert Fiveson, accused the producers of Michael Bay's film, *The Island*, of stealing their story. I believe it was settled out of court before going to trial.

CHAPTER SIXTEEN

General Hospital

There are two projects I shot that really helped to define my career for several different reasons. The main reason being they were both answers the prayer of a seven-year old girl who had once dreamed of falling from a balcony onto a stage and into a Broadway performance of *Peter Pan*. Those two are: *The Exorcist* and *General Hospital*.

When I auditioned for *General Hospital*, I read for Marvin Paige. The same Marvin Paige who cast me in *Planet of the Apes*. At the audition I was sitting in his waiting room reading over the scene. I started counting the lines. I didn't see many and I really didn't want to do a role that had less than five lines of dialogue.

There is a classification in television called, "Under Five," which is certainly better than an extra but not a principal role. So when I went into his office to read, I was a little disappointed. I told him, "I don't do 'under-fives,'" and I dropped the script on his desk.

Marvin looked up and stared at me, as if I was being silly. "Eileen, did you bother to read the *rest* of the script?"

Suddenly, my frustration began to morph into embarrassment. I hadn't read the entire script. So I squeaked out a feeble, "I guess not. Why?" It turned out there were *three* scenes, as well as a hell of a lot more lines. I apologized, picked up the script from his desk and then quietly sat back down and proceeded to read.

When we were done, he told me he wanted me to read for the producer, Gloria Monty, the head writer, Pat Falken Smith, and several of the show's directors. I was ecstatic that he wanted me to read again for the *General Hospital* biggies. Hell, I was still happy he hadn't sent me out of his office after bitching about the under-five stuff. And as I danced gleefully from his office, happy he hadn't kicked me out upon slamming the script on his desk, I had a feeling my luck was about to change.

Reading for the Bigs

All I was told about my character, "Sarah," was that she is a young girl confined to a mental institution because she felt responsible for her friend's death, which was caused by a boating accident. Sarah had developed a self-imposed responsibility over her friend's death out of confusion about why her friend had died but she herself had survived.

Was this part written for me? I kept thinking. I mean, my sister Marianne hadn't died, but all those years I'd spent as a child wondering why God (or whoever may be holding the strings) had inflicted such an ailment on her and not me. It was the same logic and guilt the character of Sarah had experienced. In my mind, Sarah had decided she would never grow up. She wanted to remain a kid for her entire life. That way she wouldn't have any of the responsibilities that adults have. She certainly wouldn't have to continue to feel responsible for the death of her best friend.

I went to see my acting coach, Don Hotton, soon after I'd read for Marvin. I'd only met Don recently but he had quickly established himself as my personal hero. Simply put--I thought I knew what acting was *before* I met Don. I thought I had it all figured out. But one day, during a time when my confidence was incredibly shaky, I began to think maybe I'd just gotten lucky all these years. Or maybe I was just instinctive. Maybe I didn't really know what acting was at all. That's when I found Don.

Don Hotton taught me a technique to use whenever I was unsure of what I was doing. He said it is the responsibility of the actor to *only* represent the writer. Do what the writer wrote. With Don's help, I learned how to figure out what the writer wanted to convey.

Don also suggested I make Sarah as "normal" as possible. He thought Sarah would appear crazier if she quickly went from one emotion to another, much like a child does. This is what the writers originally wrote and as they got to know me they would write more and more of these emotional changes into the script, and Sarah appeared to be crazier and crazier.

Don also felt the whole reason actors study acting is so they can get back to a point when (again, much like children) they believe in everything they create. Like an imaginary friend or imaginary rooms. According to Don, it's up to the actor to totally believe the circumstances his/her character are in, as well as to know it's make-believe so when the director yells, "Cut!" it's back to reality.

When I went in to audition in front of Gloria, Pat and the directors, I brought a Raggedy Ann doll with me. I didn't have any explanation for it. I just felt that Sarah seemed like someone who needed a friend--such as a doll--so I went for it.

Walking inside the studio was nothing short of amazing. Behind the reception desk was a life-sized photo of Luke and Laura (Anthony Geary and Genie Francis, respectively), who were quickly becoming the most famous couple in the history of afternoon drama. Seeing their faces as soon as I walked into the studio was slightly overwhelming and so exciting. Below their pictures were those of the cast and I easily visualized myself among them.

General Hospital, With My Doll

Gloria Monty sat in between two other people. She appeared very focused, perhaps even a bit standoffish, but intent on getting started immediately. I respected that. Pat Falken-Smith sat on Gloria's left. She was a tall woman, well-built with blonde hair. She was the head writer on the show, and somehow I just felt there was a connection between us, like we were going to get along without a problem. To Gloria's right was Alan Pultz. He was a very congenial-looking man with blond receding hair. I had a very good, very warm, feeling about him as well.

After a few silent moments of them just sitting there, staring at me, I figured I better get started. I transported myself to the ward of Forest Hills Mental Hospital. I was needy and grabbed on to the Raggedy Ann doll, and delivered a speech to Heather about how much I loved her and needed her. When we were done everybody was again very silent. I'm not sure exactly who started talking, but it was probably me. I just remember chatting and going on and on about God knows what. To this day I have no idea what I said in that room. I just kept rambling on until the studio folks said they'd seen what they needed to.

My instructions to myself are always to get out of the room after an audition as quickly as possible, because often the last thing you say is the worst thing you say. I always aim to simply go in, read, and get out. This time it was a "go" because I found out, much later on, that my behavior side was one of the reasons I booked the job. I guess my scattered, rambling, and chatty nature made me seem crazy for real.

When I was done with my audition I left the studio and went home to see Thomas. Going home to wait after an audition is one of the hardest parts of any actor's job. In theory, you've given the best audition you could and you are just supposed to forget about it. Sounds pretty simple, right? Wrong. Sometimes, when I feel less than confident about an audition, I start picking apart what I did and I replay the moments I could have done better. Well, I must have done something right because I didn't have to wait very long.

I got a call from Marvin Paige that same evening. He told me they wanted me to play Sarah. I was ecstatic. The contract was guaranteed for one show per week with the possibility of doing more. They offered me scale. And although my heart was beating uncontrollably, I put on my most confident voice and said, "Well, I have to think about it. I have to talk to my people." In all honesty, I didn't actually have any "people," I just thought it sounded good.

Marvin took a pause and told me if I didn't like the deal, then they would go with their second choice. I didn't have an agent at the time so it was really up to me. And even though I didn't think there was a second choice, I agreed to the deal. Marvin told me they'd send me a script right away and I would start working the following week.

When I hung up the phone, I started dancing. Actually, it was probably less like dancing and more like a bunch of jumping up and down and screaming at the top of my lungs. By then, Thomas had come out of the bedroom and asked what was going on. I told him the news and he started dancing with me. He's always been nothing but happy for me and my successes. I think he's unique in a way because, a lot of men might feel slighted and uncomfortable at not getting any attention. Thomas was never like that. He never had that male bravado, that egotistical "machismo." He was quite happy with me getting all the attention. He was proud of me. He even asked (jokingly) if it would be okay for him to quit his job at the theatre since, with my role on *General Hospital*, I would be able to support us for a while. I told him, "Sure, you can just keep the house clean, do the laundry and the ironing and the cooking...I'll do the grocery shopping and continue paying the bills." He never did quit his job, but he does keep the house clean.

Not only did Thomas and I celebrate by having the perfect dinner out, but we also bought our first VCR. They had only just come out and were big and heavy. It cost a thousand dollars back then, but it lasted forever. When we got home, we hooked it up to the TV, popped a tape in the slide and watched a movie. I even had the realization that we would be able to *tape* all my *General Hospital* performances. VCRs! What amazing devices! I could hardly make it through the weekend without breaking out in song, dance, or both.

It has always been my contention that the happiest moment of an actor's career is when you get the call: "They want you." They want *you*. In that moment, everything in the world is absolutely perfect. The sky is the limit. Nothing can hold you back. They want you, they love you, you're the only one.

First Day Shooting

Monday finally came and I made my way back to ABC Studios. I checked in with the security guard and he found my name on his list. I was "on the list." Make no mistake about it, I was part of the cast now.

I walked down the steps and reported to the main offices. They sent me directly to wardrobe because they had to find clothes that would look right for a patient in a mental hospital; slacks, shirts and a couple of nightgowns. They pulled what they had and also gave me permission to shop on my own, but cautioned me to keep the receipts.

Afterward, it was off to makeup and hair. They decided Sarah would never use bobby pins or barrettes because she could easily hurt herself or someone else with them. So they used covered rubber bands and Sarah often wore little girl bunches or braids.

For my makeup, I told them I didn't want to be made up like most Soap Opera actresses, all perfect and beautiful. All I wanted was a base makeup, some blush and a little mascara. The makeup people grew to love me because, what would normally be at least a full hour-long makeup session for a soap star, was only fifteen-minutes for me. Then there was nothing left to do except pick up my script, go home and wait for my call for the next day.

Because my character was being introduced for the first time, there were about twenty pages of lines to learn. *I can do this easily*, I thought. Don Hotton had taught me that when you have a lot of lines, figure out what the character wants to say, in your own words. Then, when you understand the material, go back and get the words right. Thomas would help run lines with me too. He would read the cues of all the other parts and I would act my lines.

So the call had come to go to work on that Tuesday. I was assigned to my dressing room that I shared with an actress named Susan Pratt (aka Susan O'Hanlon). I put on my wardrobe, which fit nicely, and added a pair of socks. I made sure Sarah always wore socks because hospitals are cold (during any given episode, one would often see Sarah get into bed and catch a glimpse of her dirty floor-stained socks). After getting dressed, I went to makeup and fifteen minutes later, I was ready to shoot. But first, I had to have a meeting with the intimidating Gloria Monty.

I hadn't spoken with Gloria since my audition and was more than a bit nervous as to why she would want or need to meet with me, so I timidly walked to her office--a small room, fairly dark, lit only by a small lamp in the corner. At first she was cordial and sweet. She gestured me toward a chair and welcomed me to the show. She told me how nice it was to have me there. Then she hit me with two barrels: "No overacting here, Eileen," she glared at me. "We simply will have no overacting." I felt the blood in my head go clear down to my toes. "We will be watching you closely," she said. Then she got up and left. That was it.

I sat in the room alone for a few minutes. When I finally stood up, I was shaking, on the verge of tears. For a moment, I felt like that little kid again, the one who silently returned a confused look when my mother told me I could only be an actress, "if I was good." But this time I didn't let that demon get me. I straightened my cotton shirt and shapeless pants and said to myself, *I will show you*, and marched out of the room.

I later found out Gloria greeted all the new women to the show like that. Not the men, though. She always had a soft spot for the men on the show, including the likes of Richard Dean Anderson, Doug Sheen, and of course Tony Geary. But she would find the weak spot in all the actresses and use it to her advantage. And although I tried not to show it, it worked on me.

The day I shot my first episode I was anxious. This was the most popular soap opera ever, a show that reached twelve-million viewers. The last thing I wanted to do was mess up. I remember one of the other actors telling me, "If you hear

269

Gloria's high heels clicking on the floors, it means someone is in trouble." She and the director would stay in the booth and watch the shoot from a bank of monitors. On more than one occasion, I *do* remember the door to the booth swinging open, the sound of those heels getting louder and louder like the second hand of a clock ticking down, warning me my time on the show was about to expire.

The scene went fantastic and Gloria never came out of the booth once. I was so excited, relieved, happy, all at once. When I told Thomas about it, he said something I will always remember: "Do your work, play your character and don't worry about things you can't control. And most of all have fun." And boy did I.

I did most of my scenes with Robin Matson, who played Heather. For the most part, our characters were alone in the mental hospital. Sometimes Doug Sheen came to visit. He played "Joe," the Port Charles head detective who was trying to figure out who killed Heather's former friend Diana Taylor. Early on in their relationship when our characters first meet, Heather confides in Sarah that she had killed Diana with a dose of acid and a gun. Sarah develops a huge friendly crush on Heather (It was completely non-sexual. She simply needed to be loved and to have a friend). She even hides Heather's murder weapon in the head of a doll so Heather will never leave her.

Our scenes were almost always just two-people. And we always shot last because if the show was running late and in danger of going into overtime, they knew we would shoot fast.

In the beginning, Robin and I were very nervous about going last. We'd spend most of the days going over our lines so we would know them cold when it came time to shoot. The only actors who were allowed to use cue boards or dummy boards were the older actors. We, on the other hand, were subject to a tongue-lashing if it even appeared like we were eyeing the boards (it is imperative that you know your lines as written by the writers so the cameras know where to move with your actions). After a while though, shooting last became real easy. You see, the brain is like a muscle. And, like any other muscle, the more you use it--in this case, to memorize a lot of lines--the easier it becomes.

All other afternoon dramas are shot like a one-hour play. They rehearse scene-by-scene in the morning, then do a dress rehearsal, and then shoot scene-by-scene until the end. *General Hospital* was very different than most and was actually shot like a film. They would shoot all the scenes involving a set of actors, then move on to their next scenes. Some actors would come in really early in the morning, seven a.m., and be out right after lunch. This was another perk about shooting last because, having never been an early bird, we would generally arrive around eleven a.m., do a blocking rehearsal, have lunch, shoot a dress rehearsal, and then we would shoot the one hour episode and finish up around seven p.m..

Sarah was a fabulous character. She was sweet and pitiful but she was also manipulative and cunning. She was mixed up, confused. Alternatively, Heather was a psychopath, or so my fans thought. On the other hand, fans of Heather felt Sarah was a num-nut. And they really showed their support by writing fan letters to the show and also separately to Robin and me. Pretty soon, Sarah and Heather were the two most popular characters on the show, next to Luke and Laura.

General Hospital with my nemesis, Heather

General Hospital became so popular that the world pretty much stopped when the show came on. Whether it was three o'clock on the east coast or two o'clock on the west coast, business lunch hours were scheduled around *General Hospital*. Employees from corporations to small retail businesses would stop work to watch the show. Stay-at-home moms would rush their kids home from school so they could watch together. Sororities and fraternities planned parties around *General Hospital* showings. It was an afternoon phenomenon that had never happened before, never since and likely won't again. Sadly, afternoon dramas are slowly but surely dropping out of sight and being canceled.

For us, it was like being on a nighttime drama--in terms of recognition. Shows like *Dallas* or *Falcon's Crest* were the only nighttime serial TV shows at the time. It was very much unlike now when we have shows like *Grey's Anatomy*, *Desperate Housewives*, *Lost*, and the late (and missed) *Brothers and Sisters*. These nighttime shows are just like the afternoon shows featuring cliff hangers, recognizable characters, characters you grow to either love or hate, characters with loads of money or broke. But the real common identifier is that there was always *tons* of drama.

As time went on, and when Thomas and I went out, I was being recognized more and more as "Sarah." People would see me on the street, at restaurants, at the airport, or at events and live charity shows and they'd ask me to sign autographs--the same autographs I had practiced over and over at The Neighborhood Playhouse. Whenever Thomas and I went out to the movies, we were suddenly being brought to the front of the line. "Hey, you're Sarah from *General Hospital*! Get on up here!"

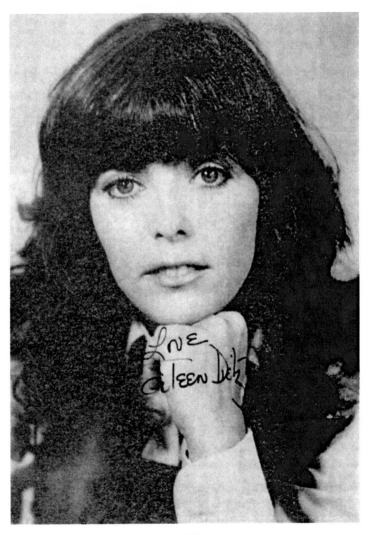

A Signed Picture!

I got to participate in a charity baseball game with the Special Olympics in Las Vegas, once. It was like no event I'd ever done before. Sarah was a character who'd been burdened by severe mental issues so it was easy for the kids with disabilities to relate to her. It was incredibly humbling. They were the sweetest kids I've ever met. My friend Dee Wallace was also in Vegas for the event and as we stood on the sidelines she heard people yelling, "Sarah, Sarah! Look this way!"

Dee looked at me and asked, "How do you get that?"

"Do TV," I gushed. Deep down, I couldn't believe the woman who played Dudley Moore's love interest in *Ten* and the Mom in *ET* was asking *me* how I got this kind of recognition.

Me and Dee Wallace at the Special Olympics

Me and Cher and a Lovely Actress Emily McCloughlin

I was so happy. I was finally receiving attention and recognition for doing something good. I'd always dreamed of being on a television interview show and here I was, being invited to Regis Philbin, the Los Angeles and New York morning shows, and several cable shows. I had fun seeing myself on the monitor as they ran a couple of my scenes, just as I had seen so many actors do.

It was great being back home in New York because, although *General Hospital* was shot on the west coast, practically every other soap was, and still is, shot in New York. Being recognized in my home state as "Sarah from *General Hospital*" was literally a dream come true.

Heels Clicking

One day, I heard the infamous clicking of Gloria's heels when she came out to "get me" right before we shot a big scene. For the scene I'm supposed to perform this huge meltdown after Heather threatens to tell on Sarah for killing her best friend. After her meltdown, Sarah would fall into a coma. However, prior to my "meltdown" scene, I heard the unrelenting "click-click-click" of Gloria's heels as she came out of the booth and marched over to me. She looked at me with that stare she had and said, "Eileen, this is a BIG scene. Do NOT overact!" And I didn't.

We shot the scene in very little time and it was great. I was extremely pleased with my performance and I suppose Gloria was too because she never came back out of the booth. The fans kept showing their support by sending letters and I ended up staying longer than I'd expected.

Of course, my time on *General Hospital* did eventually come to an end, but not like I'd hoped.

CHAPTER SEVENTEEN

A Psychic and a Shark

On a seemingly harmless, sunny Sunday afternoon, while Thomas and I were watching football in the living room of our new home, the phone rang. It was Sue Factor, my PR agent. She told me there was a radio station that was getting ready to record a show and they wanted me to do it. I suppose someone had dropped out and thus they called me at the last minute. Since I was already very cozy and didn't want to work after being on the set of *General Hospital* for four days, I said, "No thank you." But Sue persisted.

"It's radio," she said. "You won't even have to get dressed up!"

She told me it was very close to my house and that the whole thing would only take about an hour. I told Thomas the scoop and he encouraged me to go, but only if I wanted to. Well, my ego and my inability to say no took hold and I said, "Okay."

I drove to the radio station, which was only six blocks from our home. When I got there, Mickey Rooney was there with his wife, as well as a woman named Stephanie Courtney and her husband, Peter Hurkos. Peter was a psychic. And along with being his wife, Stephanie was also his manager.

As soon as I arrived, Peter and Stephanie began to seduce me rather quickly with all kinds of compliments and praise of my career. Stephanie said she wanted to be my manager. She said Peter could do a "reading," the outcome of which would prove that the three of us were meant to be together. I was thrilled to hear they wanted to help me and I naively accepted their offer to meet again in about a week to discuss the terms of our agreement.

A week later, Thomas and I met Stephanie and Peter at their house in Studio City. Peter was a house painter from Holland. The story was he had been painting one day when he fell off a tall ladder, injured his head very badly, and lost consciousness. When he awoke from a coma, weeks later, he claimed to see visions of the future.

Peter was a sweet, humble man. Older than Stephanie, and far more reserved than she. Contrarily, Stephanie, quite simply, was a shark. She had a knack for finding "vulnerable" actors. Ones with no management or agent. At the time, I had no representation and I wasn't sure when my time with *General Hospital* would come to an end and I fell for their ruse.

Peter told me he saw me staying on *General Hospital* for a long time. He claimed I would become very successful with the show and made other prophecies of my future fame. Suddenly, I felt that familiar, "God nudge" in my gut. But, just as I'd done in the past, I ignored that nudge and I signed a contract with Stephanie. I even had a good friend who was an attorney look at the contract.

He said, "Eileen, stay away from them. They are no good for you. We will find you an agent."

But Peter is psychic! I thought. I felt he knew what was in front of me and somehow it seemed if I didn't follow his advice, then I was in mortal danger.

Final Farewell

The writers at *General Hospital* loved the Sarah character and they wanted to keep her around, but they admitted to having contract problems. The show's head writer, Pat Falken Smith, and her entire staff were going to walk if their contract demands weren't met. This didn't bode well for me. And it didn't help that Gloria Monty had never been a fan of mine. In fact, the phenomenon that became "Sarah and Heather" was never meant to happen. I was only supposed to be someone to listen to Heather--like a sounding board--so the audience would know what Heather was up to. Thus I never did a screen test. Gloria never "created" a character out of Sarah. Sarah simply became a hit with the audience and the writers continued to feed the fans' desires. And although actors were never allowed to break a contract, the network and the producers ultimately had the right to move the show in any direction they deemed necessary, even if meant letting go of an actor.

Every thirteen weeks, the show was able to release anyone from his/her contract. So, around week twelve-and-a-half, actors would get nervous. Even if you lasted through all thirteen weeks they could always release you from your contract, which is what happened with me.

The other actors were sure I wouldn't be let go due to the fact that Sarah had been given a last name. Sarah didn't have a last name when I started on the show, so later on when Sarah became "Sarah Abbott." Members of the cast told me it was a sign I would stay on the show.

Also, actors never got to look at the scripts until the week a particular scene was shot. However, the wardrobe people needed to know the script a couple weeks in advance in order to shop accordingly for wardrobe for all the actors on the show. Thus, advance scripts were put in the costume room. All the actors knew this so they would sneak into wardrobe to find out what was happening with their characters. Unfortunately, the advance scripts in the costume room portended the "end" of Sarah, but not a death.

The writers finally walked and little Sarah was done.

Sarah was to get out of the mental hospital. Finally cured of her mental illness, she would walk out of Port Charles, never to return. Sarah finally revealed to Joe what she'd known about Heather the whole time; that she's a murderess. We talked around a fountain in a park in Port Charles and Joe gave Sarah a paper boat. The final scene took place in the famous Rose's Diner. Loanne Bishop played Rose. We actually became good friends. When Loanne's contract was up they wanted her back but she said she wanted to explore what was out there and left. I never could understand that. I would've stayed on the show until they carried me out feet first.

For my last scene on the show, Sarah and Heather shared their final goodbyes. I finally got to wear "normal" clothes--a one-piece pant suit. It was much nicer than the usual mental hospital garb I was used to. The makeup people even put me in full makeup. And when Sarah walked out of Port Charles for the last time, the tears on screen were real. I was leaving my second family, my wonderful place of employment, my joy, my bliss.

I was again between agents.

And there was Stephanie and Peter, put there by the mischievous demon that always seemed to run my life. They were full of promises and visions of catching a falling star and casting her right back out into the sky.

Stephanie and Peter: The Dynamic Duo

Stephanie was conniving and manipulative. One could assume the whole thing with her and Peter was a complete scam. Stephanie preyed on the weak. Peter was the side show-- the bait. And when he foretold people of their "future," Stephanie would sign them on as clients.

In all fairness, Stephanie created a million-dollar career for Peter. He did seem to be able to look into the future by dissecting the past and worked with many police departments to find missing people, murderers, talk to the dead, etc. So I suppose he served a great purpose for those in grief and in pain. Stephanie put him on TV shows and created events where he would shine--finding a pocket watch someone had lost, or answering audience questions about their passed loved ones.

Maybe Peter was a psychic, maybe not, but I really believe he was an amazing mind reader and, given certain clues and body language, he knew what you were thinking. I wanted reassurance. He told me *General Hospital* would offer me a long contract. He said they were talking about keeping me on the show. Stephanie told me she knew all these producers and directors and she would move my career along. I believe now she hardly knew anyone. And the people she *did* know didn't like her

She did manage to introduce me to a couple commercial agents who I really liked, but commercial agents only submit you for TV commercials, not shows or films. And, although I signed with all of them, *none* of them ever had anything good to say about her. It was very much similar to what happened with my ex-husband Richard. Everyone warned me to stay away from her and I simply didn't.

Once, Stephanie convinced me to go blonde. The only problem was she didn't tell any of the casting directors or my agents. I went to a commercial audition and the casting director was angry because she was looking for a brunette, and had expected one. She discussed her disappointment with the agency and two weeks later I received a letter notifying me that I was being dropped.

Stephanie also set up a meeting with a wonderful mid-sized agent who really liked me and thought we could do great things together. But there was also another agent who wanted me. They were a *bigger* agency. They also represented Dee Wallace. Deep down, I felt I just *had* to go with them. I thought, *Look how well Dee is doing!* I wanted to be where Dee was, so I signed with the bigger agency.

It turned out the big agency specialized in films and foreign actors. They had no idea what to do with a Soap Opera star (I had no idea of what a star I was). When I called them, I would say, "Hi, this is Eileen," and they would say, "Eileen who?" I eventually left the agency having never been submitted for a single role during my time with them.

Stephanie did get me one television show. A *Trapper John* episode, where the highlight of which was working with Jennifer Jason Leigh, an actress I have always admired. Working with Gregory Harrison was fun, too. It wasn't a very big role. It involved me singing a hymn (I don't sing), and walking down a muddy hill with shoes that were too big. But the size of the role didn't matter. All that mattered was I was in front of a camera again.

After *Trapper John,* things then went from bad to worse. I finally dropped Stephanie as my manager, signed with a new agent, then another. And suddenly, because in Hollywood you are only as good as your last job, I couldn't get hired, much less an audition, for anything. I found myself *assisting* my last agent. One day I saw him stuffing pictures and resumes into an envelope, some that were hardly right for the part for which they were being submitted. I looked around at the office and wondered, *What the hell am I doing?* I decided to leave.

I left acting. I was tired, tired of trying so hard and tired of making bad choices. Tired of always having to start over.

For the first time since I was sixteen, I couldn't do it anymore. I couldn't even try. And most of all, I couldn't take any more self-perpetrated disappointment. I was just too tired. I felt beaten and pushed down by the hand of Hollywood. Looking back, it saddens me that I was unable to be content with representation by a "mid-sized agency." I wasn't content unless I was chasing Dee, chasing the BIG agencies. If I'd only known better. If I'd only listened to my God nudge.

But I also knew something else. That little flat-chested girl with those buck teeth and big eyes, the one who said she wanted to be an actress, *had* actually succeeded. She had really made it. She had done a Tony-nominated play with Tony Perkins. She was in the most famous horror film of all time, the scariest movie ever made. She had appeared in the second-highest rated television miniseries, of all time. Plus, starred in the number one soap opera, of all time.

I had decided, if I never worked again, I had a resume that I was damn proud of. I had proved everyone wrong--my parents, my teachers, my friends. I was an amazing success. The little kid from Queens-by-way-of Manhattan had indeed made it against all odds. I could hold my head high. No matter what, I was still an actress. Even if I never made another movie like *The Exorcist*; even if I never again got to be a part of a wonderful show like *General Hospital, Korg* or *Planet of the Apes*; and even if I never got to be in another stage show like *Steambath* or *Ontological Proof of My Existence*, I was still an actress.

I *am* an actress.

CHAPTER EIGHTEEN
New Beginnings

Family Ties

I'm happy to say that ultimately my mother did find her independence. After my father passed away, she spent the next fifteen years living alone in Miami like a little sprite amongst the rich dames of southern Florida who did nothing all day except gossip and play canasta. They never cared for my mom. They always made fun of her colored, playful sneakers and her bubbly persona.

Mom only had one really close friend in Florida. When that friend passed on, my mom told me, "One of the worst things about growing old is that all your friends die off." A sad way to look at life, but nonetheless true.

Once, mom went half-way around the world on a freighter to visit the pyramids of Egypt, and then to India. She did it all by herself and really enjoyed her freedom of being able to see the world on her own terms. After that, her health began to deteriorate and I went down to Florida for six weeks to take care of her. And then, at the insistence of her doctors, I moved her to Los Angeles with me. A part of me feels the doctors just wanted to get rid of another old person, but I dutifully took her to Los Angeles. Three weeks later, she passed on.

We became really close those last couple of years. To this day, I still miss her. Usually when something good happens, or, when something *bad* happens. Even when I'm sick and I just want my mommy.

Deni married young. She found a man named Art who was very good at pushing her around. He yelled and Deni jumped. He was a hypochondriac, too. My father would grill steaks and corn on Sunday afternoons and Art would be shut away in the bathroom, moaning and complaining about a stomach bug.

Deni supported him as they toured the country from job to job. Art was a teacher when they first met, and later on went to work for NASA. They had three kids together; Sandi, Jon and Glen. All three are grown up now. Sandi is a Girl Scout Leader who works occasionally and loves karaoke. She lives in Indiana with her two kids; Will, named after my dad, and Marley. Jon lives in Florida with three children; Jude and Prudence, and Marley (through marriage). And Glen, a fabulous rebel and an awesome musician who has a band called Hot Gazpacho, lives in Denver with his kids Jade and Nature ("Nate") and his beautiful wife Laura.

When he finally left school and was making a good living, Art divorced Deni and married a woman who possessed nothing even resembling a creative streak. After the hurt finally wore off, Deni took some comfort in believing this woman would at least help to provide a stable home for her kids. Unfortunately, she turned out to be a bitch on wheels and tried to turn Deni's kids against her. The woman eventually died of cancer and Art ended up having to take care of his new wife for years as she died a terrible and slow death.

Deni married again and, while married to her second husband, decided she wanted to be an author. She penned a book as part of a series entitled, *Throw Darts at a Cheesecake.* After that she wrote, *Fifty Cents for Your Soul,* which was inspired by *The Exorcist.* In fact, the first half-dozen or so chapters are a not-entirely-fictionalized version of how I got the role.

These days, Deni has since remarried again and lives on Vancouver Island with her husband, writer Gordon Aalborg. They met online and, in a very unique and romantic courtship, co-wrote a book called, *Poetry in E-Motion.* She went to meet him in Australia, where he lived at the time, and eventually they fell in love, moved back to the United States and then ultimately settled into a house in Vancouver.

My twin sister, Marianne, opened her own business, Top Jobs, where she worked during the day. At night she tended bar in downtown New York City. She met her husband Eddie while tending bar one night.

Marianne and Eddie have three kids: David, Tricia and Danny. They lived off the canals of Long Island, which was fantastic for them as their passion was for boats and fishing, just like my dad. Every weekend, during the summer, the five of them would pack lunches. Eddie would don his Captain's hat and they'd set off on the sailboat together.

Marianne, David, Tricia and Danny

Their kids always found it amusing that none of the other kids at school believed them when they said I was in *The Exorcist* and *General Hospital*. They're all grown up now and the boys have wanderlust, constantly traveling the world. David has worked for United Airlines and then South American Airlines as a Sales Manager. Danny is currently traveling the world, patiently figuring out the next step in his life. Tricia has become a major force in Marketing and Advertising and now works for Fox Sports News. She moved out to California about four years ago with her cock-a-poo, Maddie, the best little dog in the whole world. She has since moved back to New York with her dog and newborn daughter, Sofia.

Me and My Niece Tricia

As for me, I never had kids. I was never against having them. I just never had the time. It was always, "tomorrow," "maybe next year," or "maybe someday down the line," until one day, there were no more tomorrows or some-days. Sofia is the first baby I ever held, bottle-fed, diapered and had fall asleep in my arms. She's the sweetest little thing and I miss her now that she's in New York. As Frank Sinatra once sang, "...Regrets? Yeah, I have a few..."

Eileen B.C. (Before Chris)

One night in November, 1999, I was standing backstage at a musical comedy show where a friend of mine was performing. My cell phone rang. I quietly answered and the voice on the other end said, "This is Chris Roe. I want to work with you." It was a phone call that would change my life forever, not only because it would begin a relationship that would revive my career, but it would send me to places I had never been before. I can't begin to express how much Chris has made a difference in my life as well as my career. He is not only my manger, but my best friend, and I have become a fairy godmother to his children.

But I am getting way ahead of myself. There are wonderful occurrences and miracles which led up to that fateful phone call.

Keeping Busy

After the heartbreak of leaving *General Hospital* and the realization of the bad choices I had made, I hadn't had the heart to compete in the business for a very long time. I didn't want to have to deal with the anxiety of waiting for the phone to ring or the pressures of auditions. I basically quit. And yet, I did somehow manage to work with friends who would call me and ask me to be in their projects. After all, I did have to make a living.

I went to work with Will Geer's, Theatricum Botanicum. It was (and still is) a beautiful place nestled within Topanga Canyon. The theatre was built outdoors and into a hill, beyond which is a small waterfall and a wooded area. It is called *Theatricum* for theatre and *Botanicum* for all the plants, flowers and woods.

Will had started the company back in the 1950s after being blacklisted for refusing to testify in front of the House Committee on un-American activities. Many actors, whose names also showed up on Senator McCarthy's list of Americans accused of being communists or communist sympathizers, had trouble finding work. So Will, via his Theatricum Botanicum, offered several of these actors a place to work. They present mostly classic plays and Shakespeare. When Will died, his wife Ellen took over the theatre and it was there, many years after the blacklist, I found myself working.

293

Working at The Odyssey Theatre

It was while I was working there that a company member told me about another small theatre company called Theatre of N.O.T.E. At N.O.T.E., one of the first people to befriend me was an actress named Margo Romero. When

Margo left N.O.T.E. she started producing and directing small films. Luckily, I was able to savor some of my creativity by acting in her films. Most were small roles in small films but I was in front of a camera again. Sadly, none of them were ever released theatrically and this was way before DVDs. But Margo was to play a huge part in my life as a director. I have worked for her many times and she directed my favorite independent film, *Queens of Screams*. I am so grateful to her and for her immense talent as a director.

While I was at Theatre of N.O.T.E. I met two lifelong friends: the aforementioned Margo Romero, and Lauren Hammond. Lauren put together a company with a former Angel and Dodger player named Jay Johnston. Together they opened "Sport Things" where they hold silent auctions for sports memorabilia. The silent auctions are always held for charity organizations and I actually worked for them for a while. Little did I know that one day I would be selling my own memorabilia at horror conventions.

Margo and a few other friends put together clothes-swaps where we women would go through our closets and take out clothes we hadn't worn in years, clothes we didn't like anymore, some of which still had price tags, and clothes that no longer fit. We would then get together with everyone, bringing nibbles and some wine. It was a lot of fun and we still have clothes swaps today. You have to hold up your clothes, piece by piece, and the rule is you are not allowed to say anything bad about your body or your clothes. After all, who would want your clothes if you had a guy break up with you while you wore particular sweater or jeans?

I also met a playwright named René Solivan at N.O.T.E. He asked me to do a play with him and Margo would direct. He said the play was being performed at a place called Theater/Theatre, which sat in the middle of Hollywood. He called the play, *Madre*. It was about a man who was on trial for complicity in the murder of his mother, having allowed his dog to kill her. It was based on a real-life attack René had read about in the newspaper. The man had been arrested under something called the Dog-Bite Law which states it is considered murder if a person orders his/her dog to kill another person. I played "Claire," the woman who had been with the man the same night the dog had attacked his mother. In essence, Claire was his alibi.

When I read the play I immediately felt a psychic connection between me and René. My character, Claire, was a soap opera actress who couldn't get a job and had to leave New York to live in Jersey (it wasn't Los Angeles but it was close enough in intent). However, what was really weird is that René had written a particular scene where Claire and the guy who's on trial are walking down Third Ave in New York City, when they stop in front of a movie theater. The movie showing in the theater is *The Exorcist*. René had written this without even knowing who I was. I happily accepted his offer to join the cast.

As the years went by, I continued to do more stage work and a couple of very small films. Thomas and I also bought a boat and in the summertime, we started visiting the coves of Lake Mojave, Arizona, just outside of Laughlin, Nevada where, during the week, there were no people except us.

At the Lake

We started out with just a tent, an air mattress, a small toilet seat with legs for a bathroom (and a shovel to dig a hole), a cooler, and a couple pots and pans. It was and is a truly awesome place. The water is so clear and warm. During the day we would swim like little water babies. Then at night, we'd take the boat out to the middle of the lake when the sun went down and stare at the millions of stars. We would spend a week out in the coves. Then when the week ended, we'd come up from the lake, dressed in nothing more than t-shirts and shorts, and go to one of the casinos in Laughlin to re-integrate with civilization. We still take our boat out to the coves at least twice every summer.

In the winter we go to Las Vegas and bet on football games. This ritual began when Deni's daughter, Sandy, invited us to Reno for Christmas Eve one year. Our plane took off from Los Angeles, where it was a balmy ninety-two degrees. When we landed in Reno, the pilot came over the intercom to tell us, "It is now two-degrees in Reno. Enjoy your stay!"

During our stay in Reno, Thomas and I went to our first Sports Book in Bally's Resort and Casino. We had done a little gambling at home with a bookie, but we were fascinated by the concept of betting on football games in a huge room with gigantic screens showing all the games at once. The following Christmas we decided to try Vegas. Since then, we have gone back every year to celebrate the opening of the football season and to welcome the New Year. Luckily, Thomas' schedule at the Barnsdall Theatre was very flexible and, with all the free time I now had, we were able to take all these trips. We were so happy (and still are). It was the first time in my life that Thomas and I were able to spend a considerable amount of time together.

The Church of Religious Science

Many years ago my very good friend, an actress named Bette Rae who is still working into her eighties, told me about a group called The Church of Religious Science. Created by a man named Ernest Holmes, Religious Science is a philosophy, a science and a way of living life consciously where one believes he/she can create his/her own life--that God lives within all of us. It takes from many paths and creates the opportunity for self-realization and actualization along an individual path that is both unique and creative. The church teaches love, "one-ness" and the use of an inexhaustible law, the Law of Cause and Effect. It is neither Scientology nor Christian Science. Religious Science is one of the many religions housed under the New Thought umbrella that practices inclusion and respects all people everywhere.

There is a saying that goes, "When you are ready, the teacher will come." Despite having grown up an atheist, and then later on agnostic, this church "spoke" to me. I identified with the church's belief in a God who is not some male figure sitting on a huge throne meting out punishments to those who are bad. I knew I needed a change, but I still wasn't sure if Religious Science was what I needed.

I also had a yearning to get back to my creative roots, which was a feeling I hadn't felt for a long time. I was still a happy person, I didn't join the church because I was depressed or lost or anything like that. But I definitely felt a void. I felt like I was missing something, spiritually. I had been producing a reading of one of René's plays and we encountered so many problems until, ultimately, I decided producing wasn't for me. But during this I met a woman named Diana Lee who also told me about this institution called, Religious Science.

So, I decided to see what this Church of Religious Science stuff is all about. I went to the Spiritual Center in Burbank. A place called, Spiritworks. The moment I stepped into the sanctuary I immediately felt at home. It's difficult to explain, but it was as if a peace had fallen over my body. The center itself has about three-hundred pews with a stage/altar at the front and a large podium light streaming in from the sky lights along the ceiling. Being in the great room for the first time, I felt a connection in my body that had long needed to be recognized. Quite simply, when I walked into the Spiritual Center, I felt like I belonged.

The first person I saw as I entered the Center was Dee Wallace. I ran over to her and we gave each other the warmest

301

hug. We ended up seeing each other very often after I became a member of the church. However, we never spoke much about the "business" until one day when I saw her nearly running out of the Center. She looked a bit harried. I asked her what was happening and she told me she was a celebrity guest at an upcoming horror convention. She had to get her pictures and other memorabilia together to take a plane somewhere on Thursday.

The whole concept of horror conventions was a foreign one to me. I had no idea what a horror convention was. I had heard about Star Trek conventions and "trekkies." But horror? It was interesting to hear about, but I was still very happy to keep anything related to *The Exorcist* buried in my past.

But then something else happened. And I don't believe in coincidences, nor do I believe in fate, or what is "meant to be." But I do believe that when we are open and ready for change, things will happen.

Back in the Horror Business

Thomas and I had since left our little yellow house in West Hollywood because our landlord sold it and it was being knocked down so that condos could be built. We ended up moving into this old monastery, previously owned by an elderly actor who had converted it into a home. Shortly after the day I ran into Dee as she was running out of the Spiritual Center, I met my friend René for dinner at a place called Birds, a wonderful restaurant right by my home. René was still writing plays as a member of the very prestigious Latino Program at The Mark Taper Forum--a well-known theatrical group in Los Angeles.

So René and I sit down to order our food and he says, "You know, your picture is on the cover of Fangoria Magazine."

Confused, I asked, "My 'picture?'"

He said, "Yes, from *The Exorcist*, the black-and-white face."

So I told him, "Oh, that's Captain Howdy, a.k.a. 'The Face of Death.'"

He went on to tell me the same picture was on a cover of a book at a bookstore called Samuel French--a store that sells scripts and screenplays and books about the making of films, biographies of famous people and other aids for actors. I thought that was pretty cool. He remembered seeing the magazine on a newsstand and the book in the store and wanted to mention it to me. That's when I told him about Dee Wallace and how she had mentioned something called horror conventions. He wasn't familiar with these conventions, but something began to percolate in my brain and I decided I would mention it to Dee the next time I saw her.

Thomas and I ended up sharing a table with Dee at a banquet for Spiritworks. I told her about my conversation with

René, about the magazine and the book and I asked her if she thought I might be able to work at horror conventions. She offered to talk to her manager about me and I gladly accepted.

About a week later, Dee called and asked me to gather as many photographs as possible, photos I'd saved since I started working as an actress. Then, send the photos to her manager and he would look them over and get back to me. The man who would eventually call, who booked all these conventions for Dee Wallace, was Chris Roe.

I am forever grateful to René for putting me in his plays and for inviting me to dinner that night. I'm also grateful to Dee for going out on a limb and helping me discover this entire world of horror conventions.

This is Chris Roe, I Want to Work with You

I'll never forget that phone call on election night, 1999, when I first spoke to Chris Roe. I was standing backstage at a musical comedy show where a friend of mine was performing. My cell phone rang. I quietly answered. It was a phone call that would change my life forever. I can't begin to express how much Chris has made a difference in my life as well as my career. He is not only my manager, but my best friend.

Chris Roe in London

Horror Conventions

Horror conventions can be quite glamorous, certainly exciting and full of stars, but nothing was as easy as it had first seemed. The first convention Chris booked for me was in New Jersey. I really wasn't sure what I would be doing or how it would go. The idea of having to talk about *The Exorcist*, all these years later, definitely frightened me. Would people care? Would they know who I was? Would I get into any kind of trouble? But, after much encouragement and coaching from Chris, I learned how these conventions work and what would be expected of me. I was ready.

The New Jersey convention was right after September 11, 2001. I hadn't flown since my mother passed away in 1993, so I was terrified of being on a plane, as were many Americans. The day I left, Thomas drove me to the airport. He kept telling me I was completely safe, that nothing was going to happen during the flight. When we arrived at the airport, the place was a ghost town. I'd never seen an airport so empty. Since there were no lines, I flew (no pun intended) through the check-in counter and took some valium just before I got on the plane.

I sat in the bulkhead, the easiest place to get off the plane in case of a forced landing or terrorist activity. I think my shoulders were hunched up to my ears the whole trip. To my delight, the flight was completely uneventful--or maybe it was just the valium working.

When I arrived at the convention I found my table and sat down with about five 8x10 pictures of myself as Captain Howdy, a vomiting sequence with Dick Smith in the lower corner, a shot of me in demon makeup with Max Von Sydow, and a couple of headshots. When I visited Dee at her table, I saw she had photos, DVDs, t-shirts and other knick-knacky things. I was impressed. Eventually, I thought, I'd have to see about making my table a little more "busy."

At times I felt like I was tip-toeing into a place completely closed off to me--place where I had no business being. I was afraid. But again, Chris assured me I was right where I was supposed to be and that I had every right to be there.

Meeting fans for the first time was amazing. I'd met plenty of fans during my time working on *General Hospital*, but horror fans are really all part of a very loyal, very devout community. They know their film history, they know their favorite stars and they follow their careers just like a sports fan follows his/her favorite sports team or athlete.

In the beginning I spent a lot of time explaining who I was. Obviously, Linda Blair was the star of *The Exorcist*, so it was no surprise most people were confused about my role in the film. I also found out pretty quickly that the trick to being a guest at a convention is you can't look frightened or bored or mad or unhappy. Fans don't want to be around people who look unhappy or scared. They're excited to be there, to meet their favorite actors so there's really no reason to be scared.

When I had time to look around, I tried to visit as many of the vendors as possible. There was one particular dealer there who was selling various images and stills from all kinds of horror films. One image--a still from *The Exorcist*--really caught my eye. It was a beautiful shot of Regan MacNeil in her full demonically-possessed state. As I stared at it more closely, I realized that underneath the makeup and the ugly wig, a young Eileen Dietz was staring back at me. I could have cried right there.

HAVE A GOOD DAY!

Everyone Loves a Little Cartoon Horror!

I got to spend a lot more time with Chris, during which we got to know each other really well. He told me about his kids and his home in Iowa. He shared his knowledge of conventions and how he goes about placing his clients and the various options for events like this. I saw quickly that he had this whole convention thing down to a science and it made me even more eager to make more convention appearances.

Me and Chris

I also finally realized how much Chris believed in me. Sure, he's a manager, and no manager takes on a client he or she doesn't believe in. However, to hear him talk about his other clients, his passion for his job (*and* their jobs), I knew then and there that he believed in me and my story. After all, he and I are very much the same. We've both built our careers based on belief in what we're doing, taking risks and seeing challenges head-on. Challenges and risks most others might deem insurmountable. And knowing how much joy and fulfillment he takes in doing what he does, I couldn't help but feel blessed that he'd taken me on as a client.

Even during the New Jersey convention, and as I looked ahead to future appearances, I was still nervous about talking about the film. But as much as I didn't want to dig up the past and relive the controversy, a part of me just said, *Screw it. If people want to meet me at conventions, then I'm doing conventions.* I quickly grew to love meeting fans and having the opportunity to talk to them, and I wanted more opportunities to do it, so I did.

The next convention Chris booked for me was Mike Rodin's Horrorfind in Baltimore, Maryland in 2002. It's one of the very best shows in the country. I sat between Bill Moseley and Dee Wallace. *House of 1000 Corpses* had just come out and Moseley's table was so busy, he ran out of stuff to sign. So, he tore up a white towel, dipped the shredded pieces in ketchup, signed them, and sold them. Fans loved it.

For Horrorfind, I brought more photographs. A lovely man named Paul Davis from London offered to "capture" them from the film and he sent me several photos. As I continued to travel and meet fans, I was excited to be signing autographs. I was also making money, but most importantly, I was being validated for all the work I had done on *The Exorcist*. I even began selling photos of *Helter Skelter*, *General Hospital* and *Planet of the Apes*.

Chris also worked very hard explaining to people who I was. Most people were unfamiliar with what I had done in *The Exorcist*, so Chris helped them get to know me.

I met the woman who was to become my assistant, Mary Ann Smith, while I was at Monster Mania. I was sitting at my table during the show when I noticed these two girls hanging around nearby. One of the girls spoke with a thick New York accent. They were both very nice and not at all intrusive, so I didn't mind them being so close to my table.

Before I knew it, one of the girls--Mary Ann--was sitting at my table helping me. She had been a huge fan of Linda Blair and they were good friends at one time. She'd followed Linda whenever she was at Chiller, a New Jersey convention. Mary Ann was absolutely obsessed with *The Exorcist*, as many fans are, and when she had the chance, she bought all kinds of stuff from Linda.

Once, Mary Ann bought the original crucifix from *The Exorcist* at an online auction. An expensive but impressive piece of memorabilia. When she asked Linda to sign it, Linda said she wouldn't for personal reasons. An argument followed and Mary Ann became totally disenchanted with, and hurt by, Linda and they went their separate ways.

When Mary Ann met me, she asked if I wanted her to help me at other shows. It's always nice to have someone sitting at the table with you, especially someone who's willing to count money and make change so the celebrity can just answer questions, be charming and not have be a sales person. So I said, sure.

Much to my pleasant surprise, Mary Ann came to assist me at another convention, Cinema Wasteland, in Ohio. It's a very unique event in that there aren't a lot of people--maybe twelve to fourteen celebrities--but it's like a big family reunion every time I'm there. Mary Ann helped me arrange my table and surprised me with a huge banner she had printed at a shop where she worked in New York. She really put herself out so much for me and didn't have to.

We eventually became so close that during a show called, *The Big Apple*, at the Knickerbocker Hotel in New York, I finally said, "Why are we both paying for separate rooms? Let's just share my room." Even as the words escaped my mouth, I thought, *Oh God! Do I really want to give up my privacy?* On the other hand, given the times of the shows, dinner, and a drink or two perhaps in the evening, I never spent much time in my room anyway. Also, one of the perks of being a celebrity at a horror convention is that they pay you a guaranteed rate for how much money you will make at the show, your airfare, a per diem for food and your hotel room. So the room was free. I wasn't giving up much especially with what I received. And yes, I also pay her a percentage of what I make as any good boss would. She's since become one of my best friends.

Mary Ann has continued to help me at one or two shows a year. It was at Texas Frightmare Weekend--an amazing convention that is fast becoming one of the very best shows in the country, run by the amazing couple of Loyd Cryer and Suzanne Pennock--when she first said, "Oh my God! I'm on the other side of the table!" She realized she was now part of the convention, part of the celebrities over whom she had always swooned from afar. She was one of us. She was having dinner with George Romero, Dee Wallace, Adrianne Barbeau. I was so happy to see her having such a good time. She's a very hard worker, loyal friend, and it made me happy to see her happy.

Special Mentions

I'd be remiss if I didn't mention all the joys of my new life. Along with making appearances at conventions, I've also been working in haunted houses.

It's kind of easy because you only have to work nights and can sleep or explore during the days. Kids volunteer as ghosts, zombies or whatever, as they jump out of these scenes in the haunted houses. The set decorations are amazing as you travel through prison cells, crazy scientists' labs and other weird places. I have several favorites which I highly recommend:

Skeleton's Lair Haunted Woods & Hayride is an outdoor haunted house attraction located near Bowling Green, KY created by the wonderfully artistic Amy.

The Rotting Flesh Factory Haunted House in Harlingen, Texas.

Living Dead Nightmare Productions, founded in 2004 by John Cook and Alyssa Cook.

The Haunt in Pasadena California, created and maintained by Ron Rogge, a terrific actor with whom I had the pleasure of working when we made *Butterfly*. The Haunt is built under a bank and is very scary (I would describe in more detail, but I hate spoilers).

Back on the Big Screen…and the Small Screen, Too

Chris continued to book me at more conventions and eventually, he got me a lead role in a new horror film. I was to play an evil nurse in the movie, *Exorcism*, with Jack Donner (best known for his role in *Stigmata*) and Brian Patrick Clark from *The Brady Bunch*.

Acting Again! Hooray!

In a way, I was getting back on the horse again. And much like past roles, my part required very extensive makeup. It felt just like being in Dick Smith's studio again. They made a life mask for me and everything. The Evil Nurse outfit picked out by wardrobe was a little tight, but I liked it.

The thing about wardrobe is, as an actor, you hate to complain. You don't want to carry the reputation of being difficult. However, someone from wardrobe had the idea of having me wear a beige bodysuit with a cape on it and a triangular hat and a scarf. It looked like something the lady of a jousting knight would wear. They nixed that and eventually found a nurse's uniform. Again, it was tight, but I was willing to do what was necessary in order to make the part work.

The movie is so funny, but inadvertently so. We suggested the producer/director/screenwriter, William Baker, turn it into a comedy, but he wouldn't hear of it. He was a very religious man and wanted to keep the film as serious as possible. If you want a good laugh, look for it on the SyFy Channel. They air it on the network periodically.

When the movie was released, there was a big red carpet screening. It was truly exhilarating and felt like old times, walking down the red carpet. It was during the screening that I met a theatrical manager named Hazel Stallon. She worked exclusively in film and television (i.e. no horror conventions) and was really excited by my work in *Exorcism*. We exchanged information and, a couple of days later, agreed to work together.

Through Hazel I booked many roles in film and on TV, but *Dante's Cove* really represented the culmination of her efforts.

Dante's Cove was shot on a small Caribbean island called Grand Turk. Memories of *Guiding Light* and the Bahamas swirled in my head as I, once again, got to fly across the country to a tropical island. Grand Turk is small, only about a mile-and-a-half long by seven miles wide. There was a huge hotel which served as the hub of operations for the show, and where we all met for meals.

I got to stay at a hotel on the beach which I can only describe as Heaven on Earth--white pristine beaches, perfect weather and warm water. And, since it would have cost the show more money in insurance to fly me back and forth, for only when they needed me, they kept me on the island for thirty days.

Dante's Cove

317

Thirty days in a tropical paradise! The best part was I had to shoot all my scenes at night so my days were completely free. During my down time, I would sit under a palm tree and read or go swimming in the Caribbean. It felt like a dream. The producers of the show surprised me by inviting Thomas to come down for a week. They paid for his airline ticket and everything. We finally had the honeymoon we'd always wanted, even though we still weren't married.

I played an apparition from the 1850s. I wore this huge pre bellum dress and a monster-face that required another three-and-a-half hour makeup session. The show was ran on the Here! Network, and on Gay.com. It was primarily a LGBT oriented soap opera with some supernatural themes. When I wasn't on screen, guys were kissing guys, girls were kissing girls. I'd read the script, I knew what was going on. But my character didn't have any sexual parts. I only played a ghost.

Many of the actors had been brought down from Vancouver, Canada. The girls were stunningly gorgeous, but most of them had never done any acting. I remember the first director (who we should just call Michael so as not to confuse him with the amazing Sam Irvin who took over upon Michael's departure) would not-so-discretely call them into his hotel room late at night. God only knows what the hell went on in his room those nights. One time (that I know of), Michael exposed himself to one of the young actresses. She came and told me, crying. Another actor confirmed that whenever this girl got a direction from Michael, he would put his hand on her breast. I told the producers of the show and, not long after, Michael came to me at dinner one night and said, "I know what you're doing and you'll be off this island by tomorrow." On the contrary, he was given twenty-four hours to get off the island while I stayed and finished out my contract.

At the end of thirty days, and after I'd wrapped my part, I returned home. To say I was sad to come home was an understatement, but there were many more exciting adventures ahead.

Next, I got to play a zombie in *Constantine*. I had a scene where I emerged from the water, dead, at Santa Monica Pier. It was originally supposed to be in the opening credits but was eventually cut. So the rest of the world would never know I was involved with the film.

I was at a concert at Thomas' theatre sometime after the movie was released. Keanu Reeves' friends' band was playing along with Yoko Ono and her son, Sean. There must have been hundreds of people there. At one point the band was on a break and I heard a voice from behind me say, "Hey!"

I turned around and there was Keanu. And this is how wonderful a man Keanu is. I responded, "Hi."

And he said, "You were the zombie that came out of the pier!"

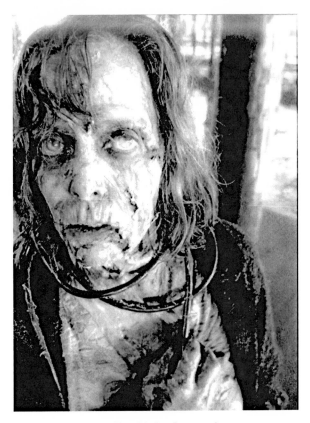

I'm a Zombie in *Constantine*

Now, there aren't many movie stars who would recognize an actress who was in a scene that never made it into the final cut of the film, so the fact he recognized me was a great feeling. Especially when Constantine had perhaps a hundred actors in it. Even during filming, my opinion of Keanu had been that he was a good man. But the moment at the concert only further solidified this opinion.

Me and Keanu Reeves, *Constantine*

Hazel and Eileen Part Ways

As Thomas and I continued to take our Vegas football trips and Lake Mojave boating trips, Hazel said to me, "Most people only take one vacation a year. You're taking *five* vacations every year!" This started to pose a problem as, on occasion, when she wanted me for an audition I would often be out of town. Sometimes I would come back, like when I left Thomas alone on the lake and drove in from the Cove to shoot *Creepshow 3*. Or when I flew back to Los Angeles to shoot a small project and left Thomas sitting forlorn at The Sports Book.

My Thomas

Hazel would get upset if I wasn't nearby when she called about an opportunity. But, after having spent my entire early adulthood staying home hoping not to miss an audition or a job, and having devoted my whole life to my acting career with no vacations, I enjoyed the sojourns to worlds outside of the acting community and spending time with Thomas. So, I needed to make a decision: either continue this lifestyle and enjoy these trips with Thomas, or be home more and ready in a moment's notice for an audition with Hazel. In the end, I chose Thomas. Hazel understood. And the good news was now Chris could work with me as my theatrical manager as well as coordinate my special horror events.

Sadly, I recently ran into Jack Donner--who had introduced me to Hazel at the *Exorcism* screening--and he told me she had passed away. She was only in her fifties. She had the biggest heart, as big as any human being could have. I miss her every day and am forever grateful for how she helped me and went out of her way for me. She was a true friend, as well as great manager, and I hope she is resting in peace.

Soon after Hazel and I broke up, I ran into an actor friend at a Fangoria Creation Convention at the Marriott Hotel in Burbank. He asked me if I would like to meet his agent, Robert Depp, with the Beverly Hecht Agency. Unbeknownst to me, Robert is a HUGE horror fan. I met with him and we talked for a while. In the end, he became my agent. Years later, I'm happy to also call him my friend. It's wonderful to have not only one person, my manager, in my corner, but now I had two--Chris and Robert. After all this time, I finally had two people supporting me, looking out for me, making choices for me with only my best interest in mind. For the first time in my acting life, I didn't have to make any choices.

Chris, now a single father, had moved from Iowa to Los Angeles with his three kids; Christopher, who was 11; Nicholas, who was 9 and Emerick, who was one.

The Roe Kids, circa 2012

The four of them had all happily settled down for their new life in the land of sunshine and oceans. These days, Christopher excels at Track and Field and knows more about movies than anyone his age on the whole planet. I am encouraging him to write a blog or a column, something along the lines of, "From the Mouth of a Teenager" and give his take on films. Nicholas is an amazing artist and has a fertile imagination and fantasy life. He can amuse himself with swords and wands for hours. And Emerick, well, he is smart as a whip and loves to run like the wind. As I have no kids, it was a natural evolution for me to spend a lot of time with the three of them. I tell them they can call me their fairy godmother.

Malcolm McDowell and Me

Along with booking actors for special events, Chris was starting to book more and more actors for film and television. He began sending me out for these roles too, in addition to booking me for conventions. I'm very proud to say that Chris' role as a theatrical manager has far surpassed his Horror Convention bookings, and he is fast becoming one of the best managers in Los Angeles. Through Chris I have gotten to meet the great Malcolm McDowell--a client of Chris'. What an amazing man, actor and story-teller!

It's also because of Chris that I was fortunate enough to meet George Romero. Chris had booked me for a convention in Florida, a few years ago. When I found out that George was also going to be there, I knew I just had to meet the man who created zombies. The man who wrote and directed what was the scariest movie I've ever seen. People always ask me what movie scared me the most. I have to say it was *Night of the Living Dead*. I saw it alone at a theatre down in Greenwich Village, after which I walked home by myself. I swear I thought I saw zombies around every light pole and dark building in the neighborhood.

Chris had thrown a party for a bunch of us. George and I grabbed a place on the couch and we watched the new King Kong movie together and drank like fish. George and I dissed every scene and laughed like crazy people as we drank. I don't get to see him much anymore, except for an occasional convention, or when he came to town for the screening of his film, *Survival of the Dead*. But he is definitely near the top of the list of amazing people I have met in my lifetime.

George Romero and Me

By the way, George Romero is six-foot-four and I'm all of five-foot-nothing, so, staring up at him adoringly, was a bit intimidating. But, he really is the gentlest and most intelligent man I've ever met.

Eileen and the Modern Cinema

Since Chris Roe of CR Management and then Robert Depp and Michelle Reinhart of the Beverly Hecht Agency took me on as their client, I've continued to work on various projects.

I shot a thriller called *Sibling Rivalry* about two sisters who, well, kill people. It's written and co-directed by my favorite indie director, Margo Romero, and her brother, Edward. We shot the film on Vancouver Island, truly one of the most beautiful places in the world, and had a ball doing so. I remember I had to wrap the film, fly home, grab my stuff, then fly to London to appear at a Horror Convention called Memorabilia, promoted by Jayne Crimin. It can be a hectic life style at times, but given the number of amazing people I've met and the great relationships I've made, I wouldn't change my life in the slightest.

There was another time when I shot a film, traveled to another of my very favorite conventions, Texas Frightmare Weekend, promoted by Loyd and Suzanne Cryer (they run probably one of the top three horror conventions in the country and are the most gracious hosts you can imagine), came back home, took the boat out to the coves with Thomas for a week, came back home and once again flew to London. I joked that I had to make sure to take the right suitcase or I might end up with bathing suits and shorts in Birmingham, England.

Edward and Margo Romero

I would be totally remiss if I didn't mention Rock and Shock in Worcester, Massachusetts. I have been invited there by the amazing Gina Migliozzi many times, and every time I am there I am treated not only like a star but as a very welcomed guest. Gina is definitely known in the Horror Convention circuit to throw the best party. There is always a gift bag in our rooms and a wholesome breakfast and lunch in the green room. There's also never a shortage of either water or soda at our tables, plus she actually pays us to just show up. Thank you, Gina. You really are the best.

329

I then worked on two amazing projects, one of which is a short film called *She Turns Back and Faces Forward at Peace*, aka *Cara*, produced by the famous Ridley Scott Productions. And it wasn't a horror film, it was a comedy. I played an actor's evil manager named Judy. It was a blast to make and I got to smoke cigarettes throughout the shoot. I stopped smoking in 1993 and not smoking cigarettes for a day does not lead you back to that awful, dirty, lovely habit.

The other project was *Butterfly*, directed by the amazingly talented Edward Romero. *Butterfly* is a horror-thriller, along the lines of *Hard Candy*. A producer of soft-core horror films is kidnapped by Laney, a would-be filmmaker, who proceeds to show Nick Cole, the producer, her small films. Matters escalate when Cole realizes the killings in Laney's films are real and the victims are all people from Nick's films. I play a religious fanatic who, despite her spiritual beliefs, puts her foster kids, one after another, in Nick's porn. I reach a horribly ugly and untimely death.

And I loved *Monsterpiece Theatre*, produced by Ethan Terra and Bobby Ackers Jr. I got to play a victim that turns into a (yet another) monster. I even did several AFI Films. The latest of which I played a woman with Alzheimer's whose husband takes her life because, being sick and coughing up blood, he is unable to care for her anymore.

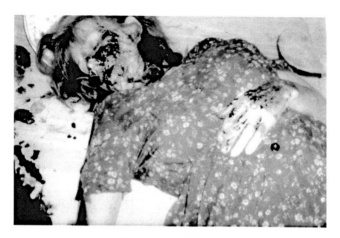

Monsterpiece Theatre

In *Demon Legacy*, which was written and directed by my friend Tracey Morse and produced by Shari Hamrick and Bob Gill, and also starring the awesome John Savage, I got to play another apparition. We shot the movie in Big Bear. There was a very important scene where the lead actress was to throw a Ouija board into the fire.

Mind you, this scene was shot indoors, and the Ouija board had been treated with a chemical to make it really flame up. The actress was supposed to toss the Ouija board into the fire, and then immediately back away. Unfortunately, she forgot to step back and her hair was burned. People on set acted quickly and put the fire out with extinguishers, but the damage had already been done. She wasn't badly hurt, and it could have been a heck of a lot worse.

331

The weekend after the fire incident, I was supposed to go back to the mountain for some more shooting. It snowed a ton and we ended up being unable to film. The crew couldn't even get to the location and they had some top-notch equipment up there. It cost all the money they had left in their budget to get the equipment down the mountain. Then it took another year before they were able to raise enough money to continue filming. But by then, they had to rewrite the script, find another lead girl…it was a mess.

The terrifying-yet-ironic part is that they ended up giving me a custom-made Ouija board—a replica of the same board that had been burned in the fire. As creepy as it seems, it was a wonderful souvenir from the set. Unfortunately, I didn't get to keep it as another person from the film came by my house one day and said, "We need the Ouija board back. A psychic told us that burning the board releases the spirits. We have to destroy it." I gave up the board without argument.

Queens of Scream is easily my favorite film I ever shot. It's *Sunset Boulevard* meets *Carrie* and is directed by Margo Romero and produced by the amazing Alex Ryan. It's about a woman who was once at the top of her field; as one of the original "Scream Queens." But she's getting older and a new, younger actress is coming up and ready to take her place. So my character kills her and gets sent to a mental hospital. When she gets out, her husband takes her to a beautiful place in the San

Bernardino Mountains called Idelwylde and creates a "Friday Night Frights" show, a la Elvira, which is a dismal failure. When she is on stage the kids hoot and give her cat calls and throw candy and popcorn at her.

From then on, every time she looks in a mirror, she sees herself as twenty years younger. Even her husband, who comes to visit her at the hospital, repeatedly tells her she's not who she thinks she is anymore, and that her agent has been dead for ten years. Some gothic kids kill her husband and Eleanor goes on a killing rampage.

Queens of Scream

She finally gets revenge on the kids and everyone who discounted her by trapping the kids inside her movie theater when a tragic accident occurs--the popcorn maker shorts out and sets the theater on fire, killing all the kids inside. Unfortunately, *Queens of Scream* still has yet to see the light of day.

I then shot a wonderful film called, *Legend of the Mountain Witch*. Alex Ryan produced and directed this film. It starred me as the Mountain Witch and my good friend Steve Humphreys who plays part of a video team that comes to the Mountain to seek out the Witch. What made this work was that this frightfully ugly creature was somehow also very vulnerable. I have always tried to infuse the worst and most evil characters with some vulnerability so audiences could relate (maybe not as much with Captain Howdy).

But, just like with *Queens of Scream*, *Witch* is currently sitting in a vault somewhere. Both films almost got distribution. In each case, a distributor was lined up, but negotiations fell apart as so often happens in this crazy business. I'm not sure if *Witch* or *Queens of Scream* will ever get the opportunity to be shown to an audience. It's sad because I truly loved working on both films and would love to see them released someday.

In *Freeway Killer*, I got to play a mother for the first time in my career. The movie is based on the true story of a man named William Bonnet who killed fifty-six young boys. He would pick them up on the freeway, take them home, and kill them. I played William's alcoholic, chain-smoking, hypochondriac, drama-queen mother. After seeing the film, a friend of mine told me, "You were the worst mother since Joan Crawford in *Mommy Dearest!*" It went straight to DVD.

The highlight of my revived career has to be Rob Zombie's *Halloween 2*. Chris got me an audition for the film and I remember Malcolm calling me on the phone and, in his wonderfully rich British accent said, "Hello Dear. I understand you are going to meet a horrible and untimely death in *Halloween 2.*" Just as I did with *General Hospital*, I started screaming and spinning like some crazy rain dancer as Chris got on the phone.

"Are you kidding?" I said. "Are you sure? Me? They want me?" Chris confirmed it wasn't a joke and I was as excited as the day I got my first role.

Rob Zombie's *Halloween 2* felt like a great bookend to *The Exorcist* because I finally got to work on a huge film again. And shooting with Rob Zombie was awesome. He, along with the other great men in my life, was very supportive and very funny. Ask anyone who has ever worked with Rob and they will say the same thing.

I only have one scene during the movie. I play a woman living outside Haddonfield who calls the cops complaining about a man going through her garbage. They think I'm some nut job, laugh at me and tell me it's a squirrel. And I say, "It ain't no goddam squirrel!" It's actually a really funny scene. Unfortunately, it ended up getting cut from the final film. But you can find it in the deleted scenes.

They threw a huge premiere at the very famous Chinese Grauman's Theatre. I originally told Chris I didn't want to go. I was so bummed out about my scene getting cut from the final film. He told me I was going and I would be proud and after all, the paparazzi didn't know I was cut. So I walked another red carpet with my head held high, posing for the paparazzi that were getting to know me by now and who kept shouting, "Eileen! Eileen! Look here! Look here!" I loved the attention and tried to forget my scene was cut.

Rob Zombie and Me

At the after party I bumped into Rob Zombie. He said he very much wanted to keep the scene in the movie, but Sony decided to remove it. Now it's one of the deleted scenes on the DVD, which isn't half bad. It's really a terrific little scene and very funny. Somehow my scenes in big Hollywood productions keep ending up on the cutting room floor. Oh well.

Among other projects, I just shot two films. One of which is called, *Snow White: Deadly Summer*. This was a really fun movie. My character is another child-like, immature person who, as a child attending summer camp, was somewhat ostracized for being "slow." She is accused of killing one of the campers and, thinking no one will believe her, she runs into the woods and becomes a hermit living with the birds and small animals until she encounters a lovely woman named Snow. With the major competing Snow White films coming in 2012, *Snow White: Deadly Summer* is really going to be a fun little twist on the fable.

After that I shot a small film called *Dark Matters* where I get to play, again, an evil nurse. Written by Robert Aguirre-Sacasa and directed by his brother Ricardo Aguirre-Sacasa, it's a sci-fi thriller about an alien nurse who comes to Earth to collect little boys who were "lent" to parents who had lost their own little ones.

Finally, and most recently, I finished shooting a movie called *The Devil Knows His Own*. This was a fantastic script and easily the most evil character I have ever played (Yes, even more evil than Pazuzu!). I won't say why she's so evil as that would spoil certain scenes. You're just going to have to see it for yourself! Also, I say it's fantastic because not only does the movie create wonderfully horrific situations, but you also get to like the people. I remember while reading the script and even during filming I kept saying, "No, don't kill that person!"

I had an absolute blast shooting this film but none of that enjoyment would have been possible without the likes of Writer/Director Jason Hawkins, Actor Patrick Green and Actresses Natasha Timpani, Alicia Rose and Dara Davey. Bless you all and I will miss seeing you on set.

How Eileen Met Dan

For as long as I've known him, and despite all the drama surrounding my role in *The Exorcist*, my manager Chris has been nagging me to write a book. Personally, I never felt like the time was right to do a book. Also, I never wanted to exploit *The Exorcist* in such a way that would make people to think, "Oh, look at Eileen…there she goes, making a cash-grab." On top of that, I wasn't the star of the film. So what business did I have writing a book about it? I decided not to do a book, or at least to wait.

Years went by and around the time I was working on Rob Zombie's *Halloween 2*, I started to think about the book again. I wondered if I could write it. Or perhaps, could someone write it for me? A ghost writer perhaps. After all, I'm an actress, not an author. Maybe if I told my story to a writer, then that person could turn it into a book?

I spoke with a couple publishers, shared some ideas, but nothing felt right.

A few more years went by and in early 2011, a man named Mike Miller--who I'd been speaking with regarding a few screenplays--sent me a screenplay that included a part I felt was tailor-made for my friend, Kane Hodder. It was a monster-type role, right up Kane's alley--given his body of work. But it wasn't a typical monster role. It also had a strong human side, almost vulnerable, and I thought Kane would be perfect for it.

I sent Kane a message on Facebook, telling him about this fantastic part. Unknown to me, Kane doesn't handle his own Facebook page--it's handled by a man named Michael Aloisi. Michael told me he would be happy to send Kane the screenplay. He also informed me he was spending a lot of time talking with Kane since, at the moment, he was writing Kane's biography. That is when the proverbial light bulb went off.

I began to tell Michael about how I'd been thinking about doing a book for a few years. I shared some preliminary ideas, some stuff about my career, "From Then 'Til Now." To my delight, he really liked my idea. He said he'd love to publish my book but unfortunately, since he was with Kane so often working on his book, he wouldn't be able to write it for me.

But, he assured me he would ask one of his writers.

My first reaction to this was, "Oh dear, 'one of his writers?'" However, my second reaction was, "Well, let's see what happens." Michael put me in touch with the writer he had in mind, Dan Loubier, and we decided to have a quick chat to see how this would all work.

There were some challenges in the beginning. You see, Dan lives on the east coast and I'm three hours behind on the west coast. The time difference presented the obvious challenge but we eventually found a good schedule that worked for both of us. Then there were some delays. Sometimes I had a shoot go late, other times he was by himself with his young son, which made it difficult for him to be on the phone. Then life got in the way, as it always does. So the talking/writing part took a lot longer than I had expected.

Admittedly, some moments in my life were hard to revisit and difficult to discuss. This created more delays, mostly because of me. Dan would email me during the day, asking what time works best to talk, and I would make all kinds of excuses as to why I couldn't talk. Either I was spending the day with my husband, going to a ballgame or having friends over for dinner. I didn't want to dig up the past or hurt anyone's feelings by writing this book. At times I would also think, "Who the hell am I to write a biography? Who am I to be telling stories about making *The Exorcist*? Surely fans would be more

340

interested in hearing from some of the bigger stars from the film?"

But eventually, we decided there was only one way to write this book, and that was to be open, honest, and truthful about everything. I promise I have done that.

Me and My Writer, Dan Loubier

Still Going...

And my career continues to unfold and move on. Chris Roe and I have the option on an amazing script called, *Lullaby*. It's written by the same Edward Romero who co-wrote *Sibling Rivalry* and wrote and directed *Butterfly*.

When Ed was in the writer's program at UCLA, his story, *Lullaby*, won a prize for best screenplay. It's about a woman (me) who wants a baby, and will do anything to get one--including stealing one or even something worse. One day, she meets a girl who is eight-and-a-half months pregnant. To the woman's horror, the young girl is trying to kill herself. The woman takes her in and promises to care for the young girl. It's a very intelligent and well-scripted piece. Chris will also be producing *Lullaby* and helped Edward with rewrites. I was and am awed with Chris' ability to "cut to the chase" and make a film so tight and easily accessible. It's easily one of the best scripts I've ever read.

For me, *Lullaby* is the peak of the mountain I've been climbing since I was a small child playing Wendy and the Lost Boys, from *Peter Pan*, in my small bedroom at Bayside. The important thing is the dream. Don't ever let go of the dream, because if you drop it, it will break.

THE CRADLE WILL FALL…

A SCREENPLAY BY
EDWARD E. ROMERO

FROM PRODUCERS
EILEEN DIETZ
CHRIS ROE

Lullaby

Chris introduced me to another awesomely-talented group of people. The DaSilvas--Wilson, Diane, and Manuel. They're film producers. They own a company called Dark Horse Films. They shot this amazing film called *Unleashed* (ironically about the history and the power of Ouija Boards) and are looking to shoot *Lullaby* hopefully in the near future.

As an actress I like to think we do big films for big money, but we do small films for great parts. Personally, I only do what I do for the love of acting. Not for the festival it might be featured in or for how much money it might gross. I simply do it for the love of the project. It's the reason I became an actress. I tend to take most of what's offered to me because I love to be in front of the camera. Once the camera is on, it doesn't matter whether I'm making $100 per day or $1000 per day. I think most actors who truly love what they do would agree that you have to have a passion for what you do and you can't put any less than 110 percent of yourself into it.

And now you've reached the end. The end of what has been the story of some skinny, little, buck-toothed kid from Queens and how she ended up with a career in show business. It's been a career full of horror films, characters on the edge, people who don't seem to fit in, etc. It was a long way from Queens, New York to Hollywood, California, but I made it. I still remember the kid who clutched her Equity card on a long bus-ride home from Michigan. But today, I recognize that person as an actress with many proud credits on the Internet Movie Database (www.IMDB.com) and an amazing star rating. One who's recognized all over the world as Captain Howdy.

Could I have done more? Sure. Do I want to continue to do more? Absolutely. Perhaps a TV series or even another Oscar-nominated film.

But who can say this dream wasn't fulfilled?

EILEEN DIETZ
ACKNOWLEDGMENTS

First and foremost I must thank Thomas Albany, my friend, my partner and husband, who has stood by me through all of this, through smiles and tears and asks nothing from me but happiness and watching football with him.

To Chris Roe, my manager and friend, who enabled my second professional life. To his kids, Christopher, Nicholas and Emerick, who brought out my maternal side.

My sister Deni Dietz whose book *Fifty Cents For Your Soul* is inspired by *The Exorcist* and is a companion book to this and who has supported me in writing this book and never let me give up.

To my twin sister Marianne, who spiritually has always been with me and knows when I need a call or a hug.

To my niece Tricia, who keeps me grounded and my nephew Danny who has never lost interest in my career, and David who still watches General Hospital and the only one I know who saw Dante's Cove.

To my Dentist, Jorge Montes, who saved my smile when others said not to.

To my wonderful assistant Mary Ann Smith who stalked me until I said, "yeah you can sit with me" and sits at convention after convention holding my hand and counting my money.

To my NY agent Fifi Oscard and Martin Gage who submitted me for the part of the Demon who possessed Regan, and to Dick Smith who made it all work and put me on a path that lives to this day.

To Malcolm McDowell for his dedication to his profession and would not ever quit like me, no matter what our families said.

To Sarah Anne Bauer who is a wonderful actress in her own right who either holds my hand and pats my head or tells me to get over it in no uncertain terms; both sentiments equally and gratefully accepted.

To Dr. Mark and The North Hollywood Church of Religious Science and James Mellon at The NoHo Arts Center Religious Science for literally showing me the way.

To all the people that dream.

Thanks to Bobby R Ackers (film producer and comic book illustrator) who has stood by me and supported me since the beginning. I appreciate you including me in *The Vengeance of Sleepy Hollow: Origins*.

I must mention Jayne Crimin and Steve Gods (a lovely, kind man who is no longer with us) for introducing me to the United Kingdom and for Gary Stone-Houghton who with Jayne continues to bring me "across the pond". Thank you.

To Michelle Dillman who was the first person to read my book and who has assisted me with everything.

To my co-writer, Dan Loubier, without whom there would never be this book and for his patience and talent.

To Mike Aloisi with AuthorMike Ink Publishing, who told me I should write this book and held me up and kept me going through all of my fears.

And finally I must acknowledge Bill Blatty, William Freidkan and Warner Brothers for casting me in *The Exorcist*. Thank you for enabling me to take this amazing roller coaster ride that continues to this very day. I know that the thrills of the *The Exorcist* will last forever.

DANIEL LOUBIER
ACKNOWLEDGEMENTS

I would like to thank Michael and J.Anna Aloisi for believing in me and for allowing me the opportunity to work with their wonderful company again. You have given this writer's dream much hope and encouragement.

Eileen, thank you so much for sharing your story with me. You are an amazing woman and I am truly honored. I know it was difficult revisiting some of your past but your courage and determination are nothing less than inspiring.

Rebecca Rose, thank you for your tireless efforts. I am a better writer because of you.

To ALL our proofreaders: Thank you for your time and feedback! This book would be in rough shape without your eyes.

Christopher Wall, your guidance and support are immeasurable. It would be my honor to be able to return the favor one day.

Jess and Bailey, thank you for your undying support and patience. You are my lifeline.

ABOUT THE AUTHOR

Daniel Loubier lives on the Connecticut shore with his wife and son. His first novel, *Dead Summit*, was released on October 15, 2011, in tandem with Kane Hodder's biography, *Unmasked*, under AuthorMike Dark Ink. His stories have been featured in Open Casket Press' (OCP) anthologies, "Dead Christmas: A Zombie Anthology," "Mutant Apocalypse," "House of Terrors" and others.

You just finished reading Eileen's life story. Now read a tense and funny novel inspired by her work on *The Exorcist*, written by her sister, Denise Dietz, called *Fifty Cents for Your Soul*.

www.DeniseDietz.com

CPSIA information can be obtained at www.ICGtesting.com
Printed in the USA
BVOW081159190313

315847BV00001B/1/P